Pg 19 - John English
Pg 23 - John VIII

The
FEMALE
POPE

The FEMALE POPE

The Mystery of Pope Joan

The First Complete Documentation of
the Facts behind the Legend

ROSEMARY and DARROLL PARDOE

First published 1988

British Library
Cataloguing in Publication Data

Pardoe, Rosemary
The Female Pope.
1. Joan (Legendary Pope)
I. Title   II. Pardoe, Darroll
282'.092'4   BX958.F2

ISBN 1 85274 013 2

Crucible is an imprint of
The Aquarian Press, part of the
Thorsons Publishing Group,
Wellingborough, Northamptonshire,
NN8 2RQ, England

Printed in Great Britain by
Biddles Limited, Guildford, Surrey

1 3 5 7 9 10 8 6 4 2

CONTENTS

Introduction *Page 9*

_____1_____

The Earliest Appearances of Pope Joan *Page 11*

_____2_____

Later Sources *Page 24*

_____3_____

Did Joan exist? *Page 37*

_____4_____

Facts and Theories *Page 53*

_____5_____

Scepticism and Polemic *Page 64*

_____6_____

Modern Times *Page 72*

_____7_____

The Fictional Joan *Page 83*

_____8_____

Pope Joan and the Tarot *Page 93*

Afterword *Page 96*

Appendix: Sources for Saint Hildegund *Page 98*

Bibliography *Page 101*

Notes and References *Page 105*

Index *Page 110*

LIST OF ILLUSTRATIONS

1. Anastasius the Librarian. (*page 13*)
2. Pope Joan with her cardinals. (*page 20*)
3. Pope Joan and her lover in Hell. (*page 28*)
4. Pope Joan (John VII). (*page 33*)
5. Pope Leo IV. (*page 38*)
6. Pope Joan in childbirth. (*page 43*)
7. Pope Joan in childbirth. (*page 69*)

Illustrations 2, 6 and 7 are by kind permission of the Syndics of Cambridge University Library.

ACKNOWLEDGEMENTS

FOR their considerable help, we would like to thank Jessica Amanda Salmonson, Jane Nicholls, Richard Dalby, David Rowlands, Ron Weighell and the staff of many libraries. Jessica in particular asked numerous awkward questions, which is surely what friends are for.

ROSEMARY AND DARROLL PARDOE

INTRODUCTION

POPE JOAN, so the story goes, was a young woman who ruled the Church of Rome at some time during the Middle Ages. Almost everyone has heard her name but her history and legend, like the Wandering Jew's, are largely unknown. Her image has become familiar to many through the Female Pope (or High Priestess) card in the Major Trumps of the Tarot deck, and others will have read about her in the feminist press, although they will probably have gained little more than an impression of an ecclesiastical cover-up, plotted and executed on a grand scale. Some may have sat through the film *Pope Joan*, made in the 1970s, and perhaps thought that they were watching a faithful dramatization of the facts. But the widespread ignorance of the truth behind the Pope Joan story is understandable, for impartial commentary is hard to find. For too many years no detailed examination of her life has been available in English, and other languages have not been much better served.

We decided to try to rectify this situation, after becoming aware that the total acceptance of the female pope's reality in many feminist publications was based on no firm foundation. We hoped that with careful research we might provide that foundation, but at the same time we were determined to be the first writers on the subject ever to set about the task without preconceived ideas, and to keep an open mind throughout. As agnostics with no strong feelings, either for or against the Catholic Church, neither of us had an axe to grind.

This book sets out the results of our investigations, beginning with the earliest written accounts of the woman pontiff, and then following her story as it developed during the ensuing centuries. We look at how the almost universal belief in her slowly turned to disbelief, and how she came to be used both in the polemical arguments of the Reformation, and as a romantic figure in drama and fiction. The physical evidence in Rome, some of which still exists today, is also examined in detail. For what we believe to be the truth of the matter, however, we are drawn irresistibly away eastwards from Rome towards the Church at Constantinople. All is not as simple as it seems, and we think the following pages contain their full share of surprises.

1

THE EARLIEST APPEARANCES OF POPE JOAN

After . . . Leo, John Anglicus, born at Mainz, was pope for two years, seven months and four days, and died in Rome, after which there was a vacancy in the papacy of one month. It is claimed that this John was a woman, who as a girl had been led to Athens dressed in the clothes of a man by a certain lover of hers. There she became proficient in a diversity of branches of knowledge, until she had no equal, and afterwards in Rome, she taught the liberal arts and had great masters among her students and audience. A high opinion of her life and learning arose in the city, and she was the choice of all for pope. While pope, however, she became pregnant by her companion. Through ignorance of the exact time when the birth was expected, she was delivered of a child while in procession from St Peter's to the Lateran, in a narrow lane between the Colisseum and St Clement's church. After her death, it is said she was buried in that same place. The Lord Pope always turns aside from the street and it is believed by many that this is done because of abhorrence of the event. Nor is she placed on the list of the holy pontiffs, both because of her female sex and on account of the foulness of the matter. [1]

So runs the traditional narrative of the life and death of the female pope, as recorded by Martin Polonus in the thirteenth century. Martin, a priest belonging to the Dominican Order of Friars, came from Troppau in Poland (and is frequently known as Martin von Troppau). Later he went to Rome and obtained appointment as a papal chaplain and penitentiary. His duties in the bureaucracy of the Church and in the absolution of penitents, must have left him ample time for leisure and study; so much so, that he was stimulated to take up that popular pastime of the Middle Ages, the compilation of an historical chronicle. No doubt the Vatican archives were useful to him in this task, although he did not always use his sources as carefully as he might have done. Nevertheless his *Chronicon Pontificum et Imperatum* soon became one of the most popular specimens of its kind, perhaps because Martin's position in the papal curia led people to regard his work as having quasi-official status, reflecting the authority and opinions of the Church itself. For whatever reason, his chronicle can almost be considered a 'best seller' of its time, with many copies being made and diffused throughout the whole of Europe. Some of them end around 1265, others some twelve years later, and evidently Martin continued compiling it until he was quite an old man. When he died in 1278, while on his way to take up a new appointment as Archbishop of Gnesen in Poland, he was well over seventy.

After his death many subsequent chroniclers had reason to be grateful to him, for they found his work a very convenient quarry of information, and in numerous cases they lifted their facts wholesale from it. So it is hardly surprising that later descriptions of the life of Pope Joan often follow Martin quite closely. We say 'Pope Joan', and nowadays this appellation is almost universally applied to the female pope, but it is worth noting that the only name mentioned by Martin is 'John Anglicus'. He does not give her a female name at all, and—as will become apparent—nor do any of the other authentic early versions of the story.

Pope Joan is said to have occupied the papal throne in the ninth century, following Leo IV who is listed in modern catalogues as ruling for eight years from 847 to 855; and preceding Benedict III whose dates are normally given as 855-8. She was of German origin, and studied in Athens before coming to Rome. After her elevation to the papacy, she reigned for two or perhaps three years and a number of months (the accounts vary), but then became pregnant by the companion with whom she had travelled from Germany. Martin Polonus, when referring to her lover for the second time, uses the word *familiaris*, which can be translated as a servant or member of a household as well as a companion. However, all of the most ancient writers who copied Martin seem to have been in no doubt as to the more sensible meaning in the context.

The unfortunate young woman finally suffered the humiliation of giving birth in the street, in full public view, thus bringing her pontificate and by implication her life to a sudden and dramatic end.

Most versions of the tale agree on these facts and add a variety of extra details to the basic elements. They then conclude by explaining that, because of the scandal involved, the popes always avoid the street where the birth took place, while going in procession between the Lateran Palace and St Peter's Basilica.

Martin Polonus wrote in the latter half of the thirteenth century, and the reign of Pope Joan was placed by him more than four hundred years before his own time. So unusual an episode of papal history, if it did indeed occur, must have left its mark on the documentary record at some point during the intervening centuries, and the question which immediately arises is, what were Martin's sources? Were there earlier accounts from which he copied, and if so how many of them still exist? Our initial task therefore is to locate the oldest references to the scandal of the woman who became pope.

First in time would appear to be the work of Joan's contemporary, Anastasius the Librarian. He was a learned and ambitious man of the ninth century, and to him is attributed the authorship of the *Liber Pontificalis*, a collection of papal biographies which in most editions extends as far as Nicholas I (858-67). Anastasius participated fully in the political intrigue which surrounded the papacy during

1. Anastasius the Librarian. From Hartmannus Schedel's *Liber Chronicarum* (1493).

his time, and we may be sure that when he was describing those popes who ruled in his lifetime, he was able to base his account on the solid foundation of his own experience and observation.

One early Vatican manuscript[2] of the *Liber Pontificalis* mentions Pope Joan, in words which are literally identical to those of Martin Polonus. However, the relevant section is in a hand different to that of the main text. It occupies the bottom of a page, where presumably there was space available for it, and in doing so it interrupts the narrative in the middle of the life of Leo IV. Details of Leo's rule then continue on the next page, so that the insertion is suspiciously out of sequence. It is not unreasonable to conclude that the account of the female pope in this particular edition is a late interpolation, probably of the fourteenth century, judging from the style of the handwriting, and certainly post-dating Martin. It can be of no help in our search for the origins of the story, as is also the case with a later version of the *Liber*, written in the fifteenth century. This one expands the text to include biographies of the popes up to the time of Eugenius IV (1431–47), and also inserts the woman pontiff between Leo IV and Benedict III. The fit, though, is an awkward one, and again there is a word for word correspondence with Martin.

The sad fact is that most copies of the *Liber*, including all the earliest examples, do not refer to the female pope. Leo IV is recorded as dying in 855, his successor being Benedict III, who was elected to the papacy 'because of his many and powerful holy works',[3] after a short interregnum of less than three months, during which a number of other candidates unsuccessfully promoted their own claims. One of these candidates was Anastasius himself, who had the support of Lothair, the reigning Holy Roman Emperor.

Some modern writers have suggested that early sources mentioning Pope Joan were subsequently censored to remove all record of her, but there is no evidence that the various manuscripts of the *Liber Pontificalis* were ever tampered with in order to delete such references. In most cases any alterations would be readily noticeable, although this is admittedly not so with a very few editions where the text ends with the death of Leo IV. Even these, however, do not seem to have been deliberately truncated; they merely represent an initial draft of the book to which Anastasius later added further information.

The only possible conclusion is that in the handful of copies where a section on the female pope is included, it is a later addition. The seventeenth century Protestant polemicists, who used Pope Joan in their anti-Catholic propaganda, were quite unaware of any edition of Anastasius' work which referred to her, and the fact that an apparent contemporary ignored her completely caused them considerable embarrassment. Alexander Cooke, for instance, writing in support of Joan's existence in 1610,[4] could only make the weak suggestion that Anastasius was notoriously unreliable; a cavil with little justification.

For the next chronicler who mentions or seems to mention the female pope, we have to leave the ninth century altogether and move on to the eleventh. The Benedictine Marianus Scotus (1028–86) was probably born, as his name implies, in Ireland, but he spent the last seventeen years of his life in the Abbey at Mainz; the same German town in which Joan is said to have been born less than 250 years previously. He, of all people, should have known about her, and sure enough, in some manuscripts of his *Historiographi* which describes events up to 1083, there is this entry under the year 854:

Pope Leo died, on the Kalends of August. He was succeeded by Joanna, a woman, who reigned for two years, five months and four days.[5]

However, the majority of copies of the chronicle do not include the lines, and unfortunately those which do are all comparatively late in date. The eighteenth century writer, Johannes Pistorius, in the course of research for his edition of the *Historiographi*, made arrangements to have the earliest copy he knew of checked. This was a manuscript in the library of Gemblours Abbey, written 'in very old characters.' The abbot himself examined the work and found that the passage in question was absent, both from the main text and from the margin.[6] Similarly, when all the most ancient editions of Marianus were collated together for the *Monumenta Germaniae Historica*, it was not to be found in any of them.[7]

When we reach the twelfth century, there are three writers who apparently refer to the female pope. The first chronologically is Sigebert of Gemblours, a Benedictine monk who was born in 1030 and died in 1112 or 1113. His history, the *Chronographia*, ends with the year 1112, and several late manuscripts of it include the following short account, under 854:

It is rumoured that this John was a woman, and known as such only to one companion (*familiari*), who embraced her and made her pregnant. She gave birth while Pope. Therefore certain people do not count her among the popes, for which reason she does not bear a number to her name.[8]

This section, obviously adapted from Martin Polonus, is usually written in the margin, and does not appear in any of the early copies. Most importantly, it is absent from a Gemblours manuscript, which there is good reason to believe may be a holograph copy by Sigebert himself.

The insertion comes immediately after a description of Norman atrocities under 853, and immediately before a reference to Benedict III, whose reign is also given as commencing in 854. There is clearly no room for Joan here, and none of the chroniclers who used Sigebert as their source in the ensuing 150 years knew anything of the interpolation.

Slightly later than Sigebert was Otto, the Bishop of Frisingen (Freising in Germany) and a close relative of the Holy Roman Emperors. He died in 1158 leaving seven books of chronicles, the last of which contains a catalogue of the Popes of Rome. In some versions of this, the word 'woman' is inserted after the name of Pope John VII, who ruled from 705 to 707. The earliest copies of the book take the list of pontiffs down as far as the Englishman, Hadrian IV (1154–9), during whose reign Otto died. These do not have the extra word however, for it appears only in the editions where the tabulation is extended to Leo X (1513) by a sixteenth century copyist. The likeliest explanation for this oddity is that the copyist, having heard of a female pope who ruled under the name of John, mistakenly appended the word 'woman' (*foemina*) to John VII after finding that there was no John between Leo IV and Benedict III. The error was an easy one to make, because Otto's list does not give any dates.

In the *Pantheon* of Gotfrid of Viterbo, a chaplain and secretary to the Imperial Court, Joan is returned to her more usual position. This work, which dates from approximately 1185, includes a cryptic note after Leo IV, stating that 'Joanna, the female pope, is not counted.'[9] Again the line is not present in any of the early manuscripts, and it is probable that Gotfrid knew nothing of the existence of any woman pontiff. Significantly in this connection, another chronicle by the same author, the *Speculum Regum*,[10] follows Leo IV by Benedict III with no reference at all to Pope Joan anywhere in the text.

It is quite clear, then, that although several records which mention the female pope appear to have existed prior to the thirteenth century, on closer examination they all turn out to have been altered at a later date to include her. In every case the most ancient texts can be shown to contain no account of such a woman, and indeed not a single one of the interpolations would seem to pre-date Martin Polonus. They are of no help in throwing light on the question of Martin's sources of information, and for this we shall have to look elsewhere.

Not until the middle of the thirteenth century, less than fifty years before Martin's *Chronicon* was written, do we start to find firm evidence indicating that the female pope was something more than a figment of Martin's imagination. For the first time material is available which does not prove, on further investigation, to have been added to old manuscripts later by over-enthusiastic readers or copyists.

Jean de Mailly, a French Dominican at Metz near the German border, is best known for his collection of the Lives of the Saints. He also wrote most of the *Chronica Universalis Mettensis* which dates from approximately 1250 and gives what is almost certainly the earliest authentic account of the woman who became known as Pope Joan. In contrast to Martin Polonus' version of events, it places her at the end of the eleventh century. Under the year 1099 the following paragraph appears, as an integral part of the text:

Query. Concerning a certain pope or rather female pope, who is not set down in the list of popes or bishops of Rome, because she was a woman who disguised herself as a man and became, by her character and talents, a curial secretary, then a cardinal and finally pope. One day, while mounting a horse, she gave birth to a child. Immediately, by Roman justice, she was bound by the feet to a horse's tail and dragged and stoned by the people for half a league. And where she died, there she was buried, and at the place is written: *Petre, Pater Patrum, Papisse Prodito Partum* (O Peter, Father of Fathers, Betray the childbearing of the woman pope). At the same time, the four-day fast called the 'fast of the female pope' was first established.[11]

Jean de Mailly's work achieved little renown. It was, however, acknowledged as a source by Stephen of Bourbon, also a French Dominican, who died in 1261. In his treatise, *De Diversis Materiis Praedicabilibus*, Stephen relates the same facts as in the *Chronica Universalis*, although he clothes them in words of his own and expresses his outrage somewhat more forcefully. The date which he gives for the events is slightly later than that suggested by Jean de Mailly, but this difference is hardly significant, especially since neither author seems entirely sure of the exact year of the female pontiff's ascendency. Stephen's version of the affair reads in full:

But an occurrence of wonderful audacity or rather insanity happened around AD 1100, as is related in the chronicles. A certain woman, learned and well versed in the notary's art, assuming male clothing and pretending to be a man, came to Rome. Through her diligence as well as her learning in letters, she was appointed as a curial secretary. Afterwards, under the Devil's direction, she was made a cardinal and finally pope. Having become pregnant she gave birth while mounting (a horse). But when Roman justice was informed of it, she was dragged outside the city, bound by her feet to the hooves of a horse, and for half a league she was stoned by the people. And where she died, there she was buried, and upon a stone placed above her, this line was written: *Parce, Pater Patrum, Papisse Prodere Partum* (Forbear, Father of Fathers, to betray the childbearing of the female pope). Behold how such rash presumptuousness leads to so vile an end.[12]

The idea that Joan's success was due to the Devil's intervention rather than solely to her own talents seems to have been first thought of by Stephen, but it arose again quite independently in subsequent centuries and was elaborated on by several other writers.

If Joan became pontiff in or around 1099 then what of Paschal II who is normally said to have ascended the papal throne in that year? The *Chronica Universalis* solves this problem neatly by moving him to 1106, thus implying that the female pope ruled for a full seven years before meeting her terrible end. There is no suggestion here of the two or three year reign as noted by Martin, and this is not the only matter on which he and the others disagree. The late eleventh century date given for Pope Joan may, perhaps, be thought more acceptable than Martin's mid-ninth century, if only because it brings her to within 150 years of the chroniclers themselves: a gap which poses far fewer difficulties than the long one between the 850s and the time of Martin. We will return to this question later.

Martin also adds numerous new background details to the earlier accounts. His female pontiff is given a title, 'John Anglicus', instead of remaining nameless, and her German origins are mentioned for the first time. Her trip to Athens with her lover, and her studies in that city, seem to have been entirely the invention of Martin, but here he surely allowed his imagination to get the better of him. Athens in the ninth (or the eleventh) century was by no means a centre of great learning.

There are, on the other hand, some points in the Jean de Mailly version which Martin completely ignores. The manner of Joan's death, by the traditional Roman method of execution which involved being dragged through the streets behind a horse, is omitted from Martin's chronicle, as is the inscription set up on the spot where she died, and the four-day fast instituted in her memory. This fast, it must be said, has proved completely untraceable.

Aside from the alternative date given for the reign of the female pope, probably the most important feature of the earlier histories is the memorial stone, whose inscription is variously reported as *Petre, Pater Patrum, Papisse Prodito Partum* and *Parce, Pater Patrum, Papisse Prodere Partum*. Although the two phrases differ only slightly, Stephen of Bourbon's alteration of *Petre* to *Parce* actually serves to reverse the meaning of Jean de Mailly's original, thus demonstrating how uncertain the reading really was. It might reasonably be expected that so tangible a proof of the existence of Pope Joan would have been remarked upon by most writers on the subject, but in fact, apart from the two Dominicans, the only other person to do so was a Flemish monk, Van Maerlant, who noted the inscribed stone 'that can be inspected at the place' in his *Spiegel Historical* of about 1283.[13] Not only does Martin disregard the relic, but so do all the later commentators. It seems to have been forgotten very rapidly, along with the other factors peculiar to the Jean de Mailly narrative. Nevertheless, before the success of Martin Polonus' *Chronicon* had completely swept away the memory of the other version of Joan's life, two further writers made use of the phrase inscribed on the stone, in a surprising and totally different context.

The first was a Franciscan friar of Erfurt in Germany, whose identity is unknown. His *Chronica Minor* was written in about the year 1265, but the section dealing with the female pope is evidently a slightly more recent addition: it has no connection at all with the paragraphs immediately before and after it, which are concerned with Pope Formosus (891–6), his successor Boniface VI (896) and the ruling Emperor, Arnulf. However, the interpolation appears to have been inserted very soon after the original text was finished and it may even have been put in as an afterthought by the initial compiler himself. The fact that it owes nothing whatever to the account given by Martin Polonus is strong evidence for its early date, and for the supposition that it preceded Martin by several years.

The placing of the section at the end of the ninth century was purely arbitrary, as its vague beginning makes clear:

There was another false pope, whose name and year are unknown. For she was a woman, as is acknowledged by the Romans, and of refined appearance, great learning and hypocritically of high conduct. She disguised herself in the clothes of a man, and eventually was elected to the papacy. While pope she became pregnant, and when she was carrying, the (or a) demon openly published the fact to all in the public court, by crying this verse to the pope: *Papa, Pater Patrum, Papisse Pandito Partum* (O Pope, Father of Fathers, disclose the childbearing of the woman pope).[14]

The inclusion of a demon in the passage is most odd, and the reference to it is not altogether comprehensible. The implication is definitely not that it was in league with the female pontiff, in fact quite the opposite: when the slightly amended quotation from the inscribed stone (as given by Jean de Mailly rather than Stephen of Bourbon) is placed in the mouth of an evil spirit, it serves only to betray Joan to the world.

There is a certain ambiguity in the wording which can be interpreted to imply either that the demon was a completely separate entity, or that it was the Pope's unborn child, speaking from within her womb. As with Jean de Mailly's account, we are not told who made Joan pregnant, or even whether it was a human agency at all. Perhaps the intention was to suggest an infernal provenance for the baby.

The supernatural theme obviously appealed to the writer or writers of another German chronicle, the *Flores Temporum*, which charts the history of the papacy up to about 1290. Some manuscripts of this work are ascribed to a Franciscan friar, Martinus Minorita, and others to Hermannus Januensis (of Genoa), but the truth would seem to be that one man alone was responsible for the composition, while the second only copied and extended it. Opinions differ as to which of the two was the original author.

The main acknowledged source for the chronicle is Martin Polonus, and his influence is conspicuous in the paragraph about Pope Joan which appears in all the known manuscripts. Like Martin it names the woman 'John Anglicus', and places her reign between those of Leo IV and Benedict III, tidily making room by moving Benedict from the usual 855 to 857. Her anachronistic studies in Athens are mentioned, as well as the notorious shunned street where she met her end. But also included is another version of the demon episode, and it is an improvement on the one in the *Chronica Minor* as far as clarity is concerned. Here, the devil in question inhabits a human body; a demoniac brought before Joan, perhaps for a miraculous cure:

A female pope, AD 854, ruled for three years and five months. She is said to have been named John Anglicus and to have been born in Margam. She was led to Athens in the clothes of a man by her lover, and studied there, becoming highly proficient in various branches of knowledge. Afterwards, she went to Rome and taught the liberal arts, and had great masters as her students. She became so distinguished in the city for her life and learning that she was elected pope, but she was made pregnant by her previously mentioned lover (*predicto amasio*). At this time a demoniac was questioned on oath as to the time the demon would depart. The devil responded in verse: *Papa, Pater Patrum, Papisse Pandito Partum. Et tibi tunc edam, de corpore quando recedam* (O Pope, Father of Fathers, disclose the childbearing of the woman pope. And then, I will make known to you the time when I will depart from the body). Finally, she died in childbirth between the Colisseum and the church of St Peter. Therefore the popes always avoid that street. [15]

Whatever the nature of the demon was, there is no doubt that the creature's sole object was the betrayal of the pontiff. Later we will see that this is a point of some importance.

The insistence of the author that Joan was born in a place called Margam illustrates the difficulty which a number of writers had in coming to terms with the statement of Martin Polonus that her name was 'John English', but that she came from Mainz (*Iohannes Anglicus nacione Maguntinus*). The obvious explanation is that Joan, although born in Mainz, was the daughter of English parents, and most commentators were content with this assumption. There was, after all, a substantial colony of Irish clergy in and around Cologne in the ninth century, and Cologne is not so very far down-river from Mainz. One of the

2. Pope Joan with her cardinals. From Frederic Spanheim's *Histoire de la Papesse Jeanne* (1695).

usual routes between the British Isles and Rome was through the Rhineland and undoubtedly Mainz saw the coming and going of numerous British travellers.

In the fifteenth century, however, Felix Haemerlein suggested an alternative origin for the word *Anglicus*—that Joan had merely been educated in England.[16] A few people eliminated her German birth altogether, achieving this in a variety of ways. The famous Italian humanist Giovanni Boccaccio, for instance, completely discounted the possibility and hinted that those who disagreed with him were in grave error. His female pope spends her entire life, until her trip to Rome, in England.[17] The approach of the author of the *Flores Temporum* was slightly different. He altered *Maguntinus* (Mainz) to *Margantinus* (Margam), a change which also appears in one or two copies of Martin Polonus. The Cistercian Abbey of Margam was not actually in England but nearby in Wales, and its ruins are still to be seen today, a few miles south of Port Talbot in Glamorgan. Unfortunately Robert, Duke of Gloucester, did not found the abbey until 1147, making it much too late to have any relevance to our subject, regardless of whether Pope Joan reigned in the 850s or around 1100.

There was yet another version of the troublesome phrase, which was favoured by Amalric Augerii in the fourteenth century. By adding one word and modifying another, he managed to produce something quite new: *Iohannes Anglicus natione dictus Magnanimus* (John, of English birth, called The Courageous). [18] But this unjustified and unnecessary variation never became popular.

Van Maerlant's *Spiegel Historical* was the last chronicle to borrow directly from Jean de Mailly or Stephen of Bourbon. Neither of their works was widely disseminated, and such manuscripts as existed then lay gathering dust in libraries and archives for 500 years before finally coming to light again in the nineteenth century. The *Chronica Minor* of Erfurt and the *Flores Temporum* fared only a little better, although a few later authors had access to one or the other. Such was clearly the case with Theodoric Engelhusius, whose *Chronicon* of 1426 includes a woman pope who 'reigned for five years', supposedly between Leo III (795–816) called 'Leo IV', and Stephen V (816–17) called 'Stephen IV'. Theodoric adds, rather tersely summarizing his sources:

She was named John Anglicus. She is not counted among the popes. She became pregnant and gave birth to a son in procession, at which time a demon in the air (*in aere*) said, *Papa Pater Patrum Papissae Pandito Partum*. [19]

Meanwhile no obscurity faced the writings of Martin Polonus. The popularity of his *Chronicon* went from strength to strength, and today almost all important libraries have several manuscript copies of it. The Bodleian Library at Oxford, for example, possesses more than a dozen, all of them dating from the fourteenth and fifteenth centuries.

At this point Martin's reference to Pope Joan needs to be re-examined more critically. All of the early copies of the *Chronicon* are very carefully laid out with fifty lines to the page, one line being allocated to each year of the papal reign. The female pope, then, should appear fairly close to the top of the page covering the years 851–900, and her entry should fill no more than three lines. Obviously it would be impossible to fit a passage of nearly one hundred and fifty words (as it is in the original Latin) into such a confined space, and most manuscripts are forced to allow her a full seven lines. As a consequence the set format of the chronicle, elsewhere strictly adhered to, is severely disrupted. The copyists, when faced with this problem, attempted to solve it in a number of different ways. One Hamburg codex, written after 1302, simply omits Benedict III altogether.

Much more drastic methods are used in another where an entire two pages are revised, with the pontiffs from Gregory IV (827–44) to Nicholas I (858–67) having their reigns shortened in order to make the requisite room.[20]

Did the difficulty arise merely because the history of Joan exceeded its allotted space? The evidence of several of the earliest manuscripts indicates otherwise, for it would seem that no space whatever was allotted to her in the original version of the *Chronicon*, as written by Martin Polonus himself. Martin compiled two editions of his work, the first reaching down to the time of Clement IV (1265–8), and the second to Nicholas III (1277–80). The latter, completed shortly before Martin's death in 1278, exactly followed the format of the former, adding only some notes on the extra years. A number of early copies of both versions do not include a reference, either long or short, to Pope Joan. They each list Leo IV as ruling for eight years from 847, after which Benedict III immediately succeeds in 855. The formal layout of the work does, of course, mean that any later erasure would be quite obvious, but there is no sign of it here. In fact quite the reverse is true: in a few cases it is clear that there has been an attempt to insert the paragraph on the woman pontiff into an already existing text. There are examples where it appears in the bottom margin of the page dealing with the years 801–50, thus breaking up the description of Pope Leo's reign, and others where it is placed in the side margin.

Since Martin took such a pride in the organized nature of the *Chronicon*, it is highly unlikely that he would have mangled it so badly at one point, and one point only, in order to insinuate Pope Joan into the chronology. The conclusion is inevitable; that the passage is an interpolation, almost certainly not from the pen of Martin, and most probably inserted some time after his death.

However, we do know that the female pope took her place in the *Chronicon* very soon after it had been completed, and that within thirty years of Martin's death the majority of manuscripts were including her. The writer of the previously mentioned *Flores Temporum*, had access to such a copy around 1290, as did the French monk Gaufridus de Collone in about 1295, and the person who produced an edition of the English *Flores Historiarum* at the monastery of St Benet Holme in Norfolk, around the year 1304. Earlier versions of this latter chronicle, which dates back as far as 1265 and is attributed to 'Matthew of Westminster', know nothing of Pope Joan, but the Norfolk copy features a slightly abbreviated transcript of the familiar account, ending with the words, 'Thus Martinus'.[21]

By 1312 the added section in the *Chronicon* was widely assumed to be genuine. In this year Tolomeo of Lucca wrote, 'All whom I surveyed, except Martinus, relate that Benedict III was after Leo IV. However, Martinus Polonus counts John Anglicus VIII'.[22] Tolomeo, along with most of his contemporaries, was completely ignorant of the handful of authors prior to Martin who discussed the female pope. He was also mistaken in his claim that Martin numbers her

'John VIII'. On the contrary, the interpolator of Martin insists that she was not 'placed on the list of the holy pontiffs'. Nevertheless, the title of 'John VIII' for Joan became popular among those writers, from Tolomeo onwards, who recognized her as an official occupant of the papal throne. A few others, when counting up the various popes named John prior to Joan's era, came to a slightly different total and gave her the name of 'John VII'. But there was never any general agreement, and 200 years later, in about 1490, the Westphalian Werner Rolevinck was by no means a lone voice when he echoed the words of the *Chronicon*, saying 'Nor is she placed on the list of the pontiffs'.[23] Undoubtedly this is the simplest and most acceptable solution, avoiding as it does the problems presented by the well-documented existence of another John VII (705–7) and another John VIII (872–82)

The greatest danger in allocating a number to the woman pontiff is, of course, that she is then liable to be confused with the real pope of the same title. This did indeed happen from time to time, for example in an anonymous history of Erfurt, which states:

During the reign of Charles, Pope John held a synod in Erfurt, while Hildebert was Archbishop of Mainz, in the year 880. Note, this pope was a woman, and numbered 8 if counted among the others.[24]

This *Historia Erphesfordensis* was compiled in the middle of the thirteenth century, but the interpolation (from 'Note . . .' onwards) must have been added some time afterwards by a copyist who believed that the female pope was called John VIII. Obviously if Pope Joan ruled in the 850s she cannot have held a synod in 880, but whether such an assembly was held by the real John VIII during his pontificate is a different matter. Perhaps there was some confusion with the Council of Erfurt which took place in 932 while Hildebert was Archbishop of Cologne and the eleventh Pope John ruled in Rome. The possibility that John VIII might himself have been a woman is one which will be considered in another chapter.

As we have seen, although the version of the Pope Joan story interpolated into Martin Polonus' *Chronicon* was the one which caught the popular imagination, and was picked up and elaborated on by later writers, there were other thirteenth century chroniclers who also made reference to a female pope. However, it has proved impossible to trace her in sources compiled prior to that century, and our search so far has not been as fruitful as we might have hoped. Before taking up the question of whether a woman did or did not become the supreme pontiff at some period, we can gain further insight into the story by examining its subsequent development.

LATER SOURCES

THE easy availability of the chronicle of Martin Polonus in the late Middle Ages, caused it to have a lasting influence on Pope Joan's history. At first, other authors were content to copy almost word for word from the account which had by then appeared in many editions of the *Chronicon*. Such was the case with the Norfolk copy of the *Flores Historiarum*, and also with another English work: the well-known *Polychronicon* by Ranulph Higden. Higden was a monk of the Benedictine Abbey of St Werburgh in Chester, where he probably held the position of librarian. He completed the first edition of his comprehensive history of the world in 1327, then added to it over the years until 1352, after which it was extended by monks of Worcester and Westminster up to the end of the century. Higden's own manuscript copy still exists in the Huntington Library in California.

He died around 1363, and a little over twenty years later, in 1387, the original Latin text of the *Polychronicon* was translated into English by John de Trevisa, a Cornishman, who was the vicar of Berkeley in Gloucestershire. This version illustrates just how closely Higden followed Martin Polonus:

After pope Leo Johan Englysshe was pope two yere and fyue monethes. It is sayd that Johan Englysshe was a woman and was in yougthe ladde with her lemman (sweetheart) in mannes clothynge to Athene and lerned there dyuerse scyences. So that there after she came too Rome and had ther grete men too scolers and redde ther thre yere thenne she was chosen by fauoure of al men. And her lemman broughte her with chylde. But for she knewe not her tyme whan she sholde haue chylde as she wente from Saynte Peters too the chyrche of saynt Johan Lateran she beganne to trauaylle of chylde and hadde a chylde bytwene Collosen and Saynt Clementes. [1]

Not all writers were quite so satisfied with the original story as Higden, and inevitably, as the fourteenth and fifteenth centuries passed, additions and modifications were made to it. The woman pontiff had at first been totally anonymous, then she had progressively acquired a title—'John Anglicus'—and, in some quarters at least, a papal number. The one thing she did not have by the start of the fourteenth century was a personal female name, but the temptation to rectify this serious omission soon proved too great for the medieval historians to resist. Their natural choice should logically have been 'Joan' or 'Joanna' as the feminization of 'Joannes' or 'John', yet it is surprisingly difficult to trace this name for her prior to the 1600s when it began to be widely used by Protestant polemicists. Certainly the interpolations in the early chronicles of Marianus Scotus and Gotfrid of Viterbo, which we have already discussed, call the female pope 'Joanna', but there is no evidence that these insertions were made much before the end of the fifteenth century. In the case of Gotfrid, his note about Joan was unknown even as late as the 1560s when the English Catholic, Thomas Harding, commented:

. . . they that in their writings recite an exact row and order of popes, as Ademarus and Annonius of Paris, Regino, Hermannus Schafnaburgensis, Otho Frisingensis, Abbas Urspergensis, Leo bishop of Hostia, Johannes of Cremona, and Godfridus Viterbiensis, of which some wrote three hundred, some four hundred years past, all these make no mention at all of this woman pope Joan.[2]

Harding was arguing with John Jewel, the Bishop of Salisbury, and by this time they were both able to use the name 'Joan' freely and without question, but they were among the first to do so.

Giovanni Boccaccio (1313–75) included a chapter on the female pontiff in his book about famous women in history, *De Claris Mulieribus*, which was written in the middle of the fourteenth century. One modern translation heads the section with the title 'Pope Joan', but this is misleading as the Latin reads *De Ioanne Anglica Papa* or 'Concerning Pope John Anglicus'.[3] Nor is the word 'Joan' mentioned in the original narrative, despite its inclusion in the translation. None the less Boccaccio does seem to have been the earliest author to suggest some sort of female name for the woman pope. 'There are some', he states, 'who say that it was Giliberta', but he does not adopt the appellation in the main part of his own account, preferring to stay on safer ground with 'John'.

If he did indeed get 'Giliberta' from other sources, as he implies, then they were probably not written ones for there is no trace of them now. There cannot have been any widespread support for the name as few people apart from Boccaccio mention it, though 'Gylberta' is not entirely unknown in Protestant polemic from the early 1500s.

Within fifty years of Boccaccio a much more popular alternative had put in an appearance. Adam of Usk's *Chronicon*, completed in 1404, was published with a translation just over a hundred years ago, and according to the English version it refers to a 'pope Joan'. A quick check of the Latin text, however, reveals that the correct reading is 'pope Agnes', a name which at one time was quite widely accepted. It was the choice of John Hus who spoke of 'Pope John, a woman of England called Agnes' several times during the Council of Constance in 1414.[4]

On the other hand, a curious manuscript from the Benedictine Abbey at

Tegernsee in Bavaria, which was compiled later in the fifteenth century, not only dissociates the female pope from Germany by insisting that she was born in Thessaly, but also calls her 'Glancia'.[5] We have encountered this nowhere else. Rather more familiar is the 'Jutta' in Dietrich Schernberg's play, *Ein Schön Spiel von Frau Jutten*, of around 1490. Despite the German contraction, this must count as one of the very earliest definite references to 'Joan'.

Clearly there was no consensus of opinion on the personal name of the woman pope for more than 200 years after her initial appearance. Not until later did 'Joan' become so universally accepted that today few people are aware of the existence of any alternatives. It is even generally believed that the female pontiff chose the title 'Pope John' because her given name was 'Joan', which is very much a case of putting the cart before the horse.

In the fifteenth century her anonymous lover and friend, now sometimes raised to the status of cardinal, was also honoured with an identity, being called 'Pircius' in the Tegernsee manuscript and 'Clericus' in Schernberg's play. Neither was widely taken up, however, and to most writers he remained a mere cipher. In one or two cases he was even denied the role of father to Pope Joan's child, although the old idea perhaps hinted at in the *Chronica Minor*, that the baby was the spawn of the Devil, did not reappear. Instead the distinction of fatherhood went to a suddenly introduced 'chaplain' or a 'certain deacon, her secretary'. No doubt this was the result of a misunderstanding of the word *familiaris*, used in Martin Polonus' *Chronicon* at this point. Martin intended it to mean a companion, referring back to Joan's earlier lover, but it could be taken to indicate a member of a household, and hence a papal chaplain or secretary.

There was disagreement too about the woman pope's downfall and death. Martin had implicitly suggested that she died or was killed at once when her secret became public knowledge, but others argued in favour of a gentler end. Boccaccio, for example, after describing how her mentor, the Devil, had tempted Joan into the sin of lust, adds that she was taken away from the place where she gave birth, by the cardinals and imprisoned. The 'wretched little woman' was then left to lament her condition until her death some time later.[6]

Kinder still, was the anonymous Benedictine monk (on textual evidence possibly named Thomas) of Malmesbury Abbey in Wiltshire, who wrote the *Eulogium Historiarum* in about 1366. His female pope, whom he calls 'John VII' and places in the year 858, attains the papacy in the traditional way, although the *Eulogium* is somewhat insulting about her talents, saying that 'so many were fools in the city that no one could compare to her in learning . . .' The monk then continues:

When she had reigned for two years and a bit, she became pregnant by her old lover, and while walking in procession gave birth, and thus her sin was revealed and she was deposed.[7]

There is no mention at all of her eventual demise, which was obviously not considered relevant.

If Joan did not die at the place where she gave birth, then it follows that she may not have been buried there either. This was certainly the opinion of the copyist who inserted a late and unique interpolation into a Berlin manuscript of Martin Polonus' chronicle. He also took advantage of the singular lack of interest shown by the early writers, in what became of the papal child after its traumatic introduction to the world. They had presumably taken it for granted that the baby had died at birth or shortly afterwards, but the copyist devised a different theory. His version explains that, as a result of the female pope's public revelation:

She was deposed for her incontinence, and taking up the religious habit, lived in penitence for such a long time that she saw her son made Bishop of Hostia (Ostia near Rome). When, in her final days, she perceived her death approaching, she instructed that her burial should be in that place where she had given birth, which nevertheless her son would not permit. Having removed her body to Hostia, he buried her with honour in the Cathedral. On account of which, God has worked many miracles right up to the present day. [8]

How different this is from the familiar account of Martin Polonus. Not only is Joan left to repent her sins in a nunnery, but her son survives his unusual beginnings to rise to the rank of bishop! Furthermore, the figure of the woman pope starts to take on some very saintly characteristics, and miracles even occur in her name. Unfortunately no other sources confirm these odd assertions, which were interpolated into the single *Chronicon* manuscript some time after 1400. The Cathedral at Ostia never claimed to possess Joan's body, and the writings of Leo, Bishop of Ostia at the end of the eleventh century and the beginning of the twelfth, say nothing about her.

The statement that her child was a son (*filius*) is also based on evidence which is far from firm. Most of the early authors who mention the female pope and her pregnancy do not actually refer to the offspring itself, but those who do, describe it with the word *puer*. Although this can sometimes indicate a male child, it was more often used to convey a child of unspecified sex. Only in the fifteenth century did the infant's masculinity begin to be assumed with some degree of unanimity; Adam of Usk in 1404 may have been the first to prefer *filius* to *puer* or *infans*.

An even greater accolade than burial in an important cathedral was given to Pope Joan by a *c.*1375 edition of the *Mirabilia Urbis Romae*, a popular guidebook to Rome for pilgrims who wanted some information on the 'sights' as they travelled around the city. These pilgrims were the natural predecessors of the modern tourist, and numerous versions of the *Mirabilia* were produced for their benefit throughout the late Middle Ages. The 1375 manuscript alone states that

3. Pope Joan and her lover in Hell. From John Wolfius' *Lectionum Memorabilium et Reconditarum Centenarii XVI* (1671).

the woman pontiff's body was buried 'among the virtuous' in the Basilica of St Peter's itself.[9] Such an honour was unquestionably conferred upon the remains of most ninth century popes, but the *Mirabilia*'s compiler was surely presumptuous in his belief that the bones of Joan were among them.

For some later writers, the female pope's death was not the end of her story. They took a considerable interest in the ultimate whereabouts of her soul, and not everyone agreed with the Carmelite Baptista Mantuanus when he resolutely consigned her to Hell in his work of about 1490. According to a woodcut illustration, she hangs there on a gibbet, clutching her child. What the poor baby had done to merit such punishment is not explained, but no doubt it was sufficient that he died unbaptized. Her lover is not forgotten either, for he hangs nearby, wearing the robes of a cardinal.[10]

In contrast to this harsh treatment, an idea grew up at the end of the fifteenth century that perhaps Joan had redeemed herself by deliberately choosing public humiliation. Thus Felix Haemerlein's *De Nobilitate et Rusticitate Dialogus*, written around 1490, states:

. . . while in procession from St Peter's Basilica to the Lateran, in the street which leads from the Colisseum to St Clement's Church, she gave birth as she had chosen to do for the remission of her sins.[11]

The theme was enlarged upon by Stephan Blanck in an edition of the *Mirabilia Urbis Romae* which he compiled in about 1500 during the reign of the Borgia pope, Alexander VI:

> . . . we then proceed to a certain small chapel between the Colisseum and St Clements; this derelict church is situated at the place where the woman who became Pope died. She was heavy with child, and was questioned by an angel of God whether she would prefer to perish for ever, or to face the world openly. But, not wanting to be lost for eternity, she chose the embarrassment of public reproach. [12]

Presumably by this decision she was thought to have saved her soul: an attractive and altogether satisfactory conclusion to her strange story.

Stephan Blanck, Boccaccio, and in particular the unknown interpolator of the variant Martin Polonus text, seem to have felt little in the way of horror or revulsion at the concept of a woman ascending the papal throne. On the contrary, they reveal a growing respect and affection for her which is illustrated by the belief of a few authors, that she was buried honourably in a cathedral or even in St Peter's Basilica. Perhaps this is a reflection of the feelings towards Pope Joan which were current among the general population at the time. Her thirst for power and occasional lapses into immorality were, after all, relatively innocuous compared with the misdeeds of many other early medieval pontiffs.

Boccaccio's fellow humanist Franceso Petrarch (1304–74), however, had no particular sympathy for Joan as a person; nor did the details of her rule and unfortunate death interest him in the slightest. His *Chronica de le Vite de Pontefici et Imperadori Romani* dismisses her reign in few words, simply saying that after her election, 'she was revealed (as a woman)'. He does not even bother to explain how such a disaster came about and in what manner it affected Joan's subsequent life and afterlife.

For Petrarch instead, the fascination lay in the marvels which he claimed had occurred on the earth following the pope's exposure. These he describes in truly apocalyptic language:

> . . . in Brescia it rained blood for three days and nights. In France there appeared marvellous locusts which had six wings and very powerful teeth. They flew miraculously through the air, and all drowned in the British Sea. The golden bodies were rejected by the waves of the sea and corrupted the air, so that a great many people died. [13]

The imagery here is taken straight from the Book of Revelation, and clearly Petrarch intended to draw a direct parallel between the consequences of the female pope's unlawful pontificate and the seven plagues of Revelation, which were released upon the opening of the Seventh Seal. The first of these was a rain of 'hail and fire mingled with blood' (Rev. 8:7), and the fifth was of locusts with 'the teeth of lions' (Rev. 9: 3–11). The drowning of Petrarch's insects also echoes the casting into the Red Sea of the locusts which formed the eighth plague of Egypt (Exodus 10:19).

But such flights of fancy were only part of the picture, for some of the other additions made to the basic account of Pope Joan's tragic life, during the 250 years after its initial appearance, had a distinct ring of truth. In the first chapter, we encountered an inscribed stone which, according to the earliest writers, marked the position of her death and burial. This was very quickly forgotten, but over a century later certain other memorials began to be associated with the story in its place. The 1375 edition of the *Mirabilia* guidebook introduces two new details into the tale:

Nigh unto the Colosseum, in the open place, lieth an image which is called the Woman Pope with her child . . . Moreover in the same open place is a Majesty of the Lord, that spake to her as she passed, and said, 'In comfort shalt thou not pass' and when she passed she was taken with pains, and cast forth the child from her womb. Wherefore the Pope to this day shall not pass by that way. [14]

The 'Majesty of the Lord'—which was presumably some kind of figure of Christ in Glory—was not linked with Joan by any other author, but the more intriguing statue of 'the Woman Pope with her child' crops up with increasing frequency from the beginning of the fifteenth century onwards.

The Welshman, Adam of Usk, travelled to Rome in 1402 and stayed there for several years. His *Chronicon*, compiled between 1377–1404, was intended as a continuation of Ranulph Higden's great chronology. It includes an account of the coronation of Pope Innocent VII in 1404, which Adam may not actually have witnessed himself, although he must at least have seen part of the preliminary procession. The final stages of the Pope's solemn progress to the Lateran are described thus:

After turning aside out of abhorrence of pope Agnes, whose image in stone with her son (*cum filio*) stands in the straight road near St Clement's, the Pope, dismounting from his horse, enters the Lateran for his enthronement. [15]

Another brief mention is in *Ye Solace of Pilgrimes*, written in about 1450 by John Capgrave (1393–1464), the scholarly prior of St Margaret's at King's Lynn (Norfolk). While visiting Rome he was appalled by the general quality of the available guidebooks, which he found unreliable and out of date, and resolved to produce a more accurate replacement. Nevertheless his *Solace* contains its own fair share of hearsay and doubtful statements. On Pope Joan's statue it says:

the cherche was deceyued ones in a woman whech deyid on processioun grete with child for a ymage is sette up in memorie of hir as we go to laterane. [16]

Around 1414 Theodoric of Niem, a curial official from Westphalia and co-founder of the German College of S. Maria dell'Anima in Rome, also wrote of the 'marble statue', [17] as did several other authors of a contemporary or later date. Stephan Blanck's *Mirabilia* of *c*.1500, for instance, records a 'stone which is carved . . . with an effigy of the female pope and her child.'[18]

All of these commentators mention the statue as an object which existed in their own day. Indeed, the point of including it in books such as the *Mirabilia* and the *Solace of Pilgrimes* was to mark it out as a 'tourist sight' of interest to the many thousands of pilgrims who flocked to the city, as a result of the various Jubilees of the fourteenth and fifteenth centuries. Stephan Blanck's edition of the *Mirabilia* may well have been issued especially for the Jubilee of 1500, in which year an enormous crowd of 200,000 people gathered in St Peter's Square to receive the Easter blessing of Pope Alexander VI.

It seems highly unlikely that the guidebooks would have given space to an entirely fictional monument, while Adam of Usk and Theodoric of Niem, as residents of Rome, would probably not have written about the statue if they had not seen it for themselves. Whether they were justified in making the connection between the figure and Pope Joan is, of course, another question, particularly in view of the fact that it was not associated with her story until the last half of the fourteenth century.

Before leaving the subject for the moment, the amusing case of Pasquale Adinolfi must be mentioned. In 1881 he devoted two pages to the female pope in his *Roma nell'età di Mezzo*, disclosing an amazing new addition to the evidence. 'There was,' he says, 'a teat, sculpted in marble, for the purpose of attesting that John VII, the Englishman, was a woman and had given birth to a baby.'[19] Disappointingly, Adinolfi's *Imago papillae* or 'Image of a teat' proves to have been nothing more than a misreading of his source: the late fifteenth century papal Master of Ceremonies, John Burchard. Burchard's *Liber Notarum* notes the existence of an *Imago papissae*—not the dramatic teat, but the familiar 'Image of the female pope.'

Another idea which slowly became attached to Pope Joan's history was the suggestion that, because the Church and People of Rome were once hoodwinked into accepting a woman as their pontiff, a pierced seat was afterwards used in the papal investiture ceremonies, in order to check that each new pope was truly male. In this way a repetition of the same error was avoided.

Rumours of the practice began to circulate as early as the 1290s, when the Dominican, Robert d'Usez, recounted a vision in which he saw the seat 'where, it is said, the Pope is proved to be a man'.[20] Such a legend might reasonably have been linked with Joan then and there, but apparently this was only rarely the case to start with. In about 1295 Gaufridus de Collone, a French monk of the Abbey of St Pierre-le-Vif at Sens, wrote that from the female pontiff 'it is said that the Romans derive the custom of checking the sex of the pope-elect through a hole in a stone seat'.[21] Yet most of the earliest chroniclers who referred to the examination believed that it was carried out not only to avoid the illegal installation of a woman as pope, but also to ensure that no eunuch could ascend the throne of St Peter, for a castrated Bishop of Rome was as unacceptable as a female one. The origin of the seat was not generally traced back to Pope Joan in particular until much later. Even in 1404, Adam of Usk saw no reason to connect the 'chair of porphyry, which is pierced beneath for this purpose, that one of the younger cardinals may make proof of (the pope's) sex', with the statue of 'Agnes' mentioned in the same paragraph.

The Englishman, William Brewyn, also failed to make the link when, in 1470, he compiled his fascinating guidebook to the churches of Rome. While describing the Chapel of St Saviour in the Basilica of St John Lateran, he merely states:

. . . in this chapel are two or more chairs of red marble stone, with apertures carved in them, upon which chairs, as I heard, proof is made as to whether the pope is male or not. [22]

Nevertheless, by the time of William Brewyn, who lived in Rome during the reigns of Paul II and Sixtus IV, the association between these objects and Joan was beginning to be widely acknowledged. Aside from Gaufridus de Collone, the first source to maintain that the chair—or chairs—came into use as a direct consequence of the rule of the female pontiff seems to have been John Capgrave, some twenty years prior to Brewyn's work. In the section of his *Solace* which deals with the Lateran, he says:

And forth in anothir paue of that cloystir is a chapel and there stant the chayer that the pope is asayed in whethir he be man or woman be cause the cherche was deceyued ones in a woman whech deyid on processioun . . . [23]

The same explanation was known to Bartolomeo Platina, the Prefect of the Vatican Library under Pope Sixtus IV (1471–84). In his *Lives of the Popes* (1479), he begins by repeating Martin Polonus' version of events and then goes on:

Some have written that because of this . . . when the popes are first enthroned on the seat of Peter, which to this end is pierced, their genitals are felt by the most junior deacon present. [24]

Platina then makes it clear that he believes this assertion to be the result of a misunderstanding, but other authors had no such reservations. After all, scurrilous material of this sort could only enhance the popularity of their works: a very important consideration in the era of that newfangled invention, the printing press. Hartmannus Schedel's *Liber Chronicarum*, which was published in 1493 by Anton Koberger of Nuremberg, and is therefore more usually known as the *Nuremberg Chronicle*, gives the standard story of Pope Joan, illustrated with a woodcut of considerable charm. But at the end of the account, Schedel cannot resist adding that 'the avoidance of the same error was the motive, when first the stone seat was applied to the purpose of the feeling of the (pope's) genitals by a junior deacon through the hole in it.' [25]

4. Pope Joan (John VII). From Hartmannus Schedel's *Liber Chronicarum* (1493).

Further details are provided by Felix Haemerlein who, writing around 1490 in his *De Nobilitate et Rusticitate Dialogus*, amply satisfies our curiosity as to the exact form of the ritual. It is diverting to realize that, if he was telling the truth, his contemporary Pope Alexander VI, who was notorious as the father of many children, must have been forced in 1492 to submit to this rather unnecessary test:

. . . up to the present day (the seat) is still in the same place and is used at the election of the pope. And in order to demonstrate his worthiness, his testicles are felt by the junior cleric present as testimony of his male sex. When this is found to be so, the person who feels them shouts out in a loud voice 'He has testicles'. And all the clerics present reply 'God be praised'. Then they proceed joyfully to the consecration of the pope-elect.[26]

Felix Haemerlein was also the first to take the argument, that the new ceremonial was introduced because of Pope Joan, one logical step further, by maintaining that it was her successor 'Benedict the Third of Roman birth . . . who truly in memory of the event set up the perforated chair in St John Lateran.'

The reality of the seat—or pair of seats if William Brewyn is to be believed—and also of the mysterious statue are matters to which we will return in the next chapter. Suffice it to say at this stage, that they would seem to be the best and most solid evidence for the female pope so far encountered.

We have now looked at all the main facets of the Pope Joan story as it was expanded and modified during the late Middle Ages. A number of other tales were told about her, but they were not repeated with any regularity and failed to gain widespread currency. Theodoric of Niem claimed, for instance, that she had taught at the Greek school in Rome, which was famous for its connections with St Augustine. That she was a woman of considerable literary ability was never in doubt, and some authors laid particular emphasis on this. Martin le Franc, the Provost of Lausanne and a papal secretary to both Nicholas V (1447–55) and the antipope Felix V, mentions the many 'excellently and religiously ornamented' prefaces to the Mass for which she was responsible, in his poem Le Champion des Dames.[27] This idea probably stemmed from the fact that several extraneous prefaces, coming mostly from old Roman tradition, were cut out of the missal at the beginning of the eleventh century. Of course, this reform had nothing whatever to do with the female pontiff.

Such perfectly orthodox literary endeavours were not enough for the German Protestant 'H.S.' who, some years later in 1588, remarked that Joan or 'Gylberta' had 'it is said . . . writ a Booke of Necromancie, of the power and strength of deuils'.[28] He may have copied this from André Tiraqueau's De Legibus Connubialibus which first appeared in 1513. Tiraqueau (1488–1558), the French legal humanist and friend of Rabelais, used almost identical words concerning 'Gilberta', who 'it is said wrote a book of necromancy'.[29] As we have already seen, Tiraqueau and 'H.S.' were by no means alone in suggesting that she must have had the active assistance of Satanic forces in gaining her position. Stephen of Bourbon was the first, but the ultimate example has to be Dietrich Schernberg's play Ein Schön Spiel von Frau Jutten in which 'Jutta' is little more than Hell's pawn, although the intercession of the Blessed Virgin Mary eventually saves her from eternal damnation.

It would be simplistic to assume, that demonic powers were incorporated into the story purely because people could not accept that a 'mere woman' might have had the intelligence and ability to attain such heights in her own right. The medieval mind being what it was, saw hints of witchcraft and sorcery in anything or anybody a little out of the ordinary, and more than one pope was unjustly accused after his death of practising the black arts. In the case of Gerbert of Aurillac, who became Pope Sylvester II (999–1003), it took no more than his immense learning, some of which was acquired under Arab teachers, to convince later chroniclers that he must have signed away his soul in exchange for knowledge and supreme power. The malicious rumours, needless to say, were unheard of during his lifetime. Joan was not even unique in being linked with a grimoire, as the existence of Pope Leo's Enchiridion and The Grimoire of Pope Honorius attests.

Unlikely and fantastic legends grew up around a great many figures, both real and fictitious, in the course of the Middle Ages, but although the female pope had more than her fair share there is every reason to suppose that she was generally accepted as a historical personage for most of the fourteenth and fifteenth centuries. Around the middle of this period she was even included in a long series of papal busts which were made to decorate the nave of Siena Cathedral in Tuscany.

Placed between Leo IV and Benedict III, and accompanied by the inscription 'Johannes VIII, Foemina de Anglia', her image was undisturbed for nearly 200 years.

The series of terracotta busts still remains in Siena to this day. It consists of roughly 170 representations, of popes ranging in date from the first century to the twelfth, although the sequence is not always reliable and some pontiffs are repeated while others are omitted or replaced by antipopes. Regrettably anyone who looks for Pope Joan among them today will search in vain, for her bust was removed in about 1600 on the instigation of Clement VIII.

There is some disagreement as to what then became of the image. Cardinal Baronius (1538–1607), the Vatican librarian from 1597, claimed that it was immediately broken up. Although he seems to have been involved in its removal, and may have been the person who suggested this course of action to the Pope, he could well have been mistaken about its destruction. Slightly later sources state that the Archbishop of Siena under Clement VIII did not wish to see the carving go to waste, so had it altered to represent a different pontiff and then reinstated. The transformation could have been achieved very easily by doing nothing more than changing the inscription, especially since the busts were never intended as true likenesses. The Archbishop might then have preferred not to inform either Baronius or Pope Clement of his unauthorized act.

The indefatigable T.F. Bumpus, in his *Cathedrals and Churches of Italy*, says that the new depiction was of Alexander III (1159–81), but he is almost certainly wrong. Earlier and quite reliable writers, identify it as Pope Zachary (741–52).[30] As the busts are arranged at the present day there is, in fact, no extra figure between Leo IV and Benedict III. Zachary appears in his correct chronological position, separated from Leo IV by Stephen II (752), Paul I (757–67) and Sergius II (844–47). However, in about 1802 an attempt was made to put the papal series into a more logical order, and Zachary's current location may well be the result of this operation.

The story of Pope Joan became so firmly established and widely believed that she was not only commemorated in sculpture, but also used to make general theological points without any questions being asked about her authenticity. Thus the Franciscan philosopher and theologian William of Ockham, the *Venerabilis Inceptor*, cited the example of Joan—although he did not name her—during his disagreement with Pope John XXII (1316–34). John XXII had issued a Bull in 1329 attacking the Spiritual party among the Franciscans, who clung to their founder's teachings on poverty, in the face of the maturing Order's natural tendency towards a comfortable institutionalism. The Spirituals had been producing tractates aimed against the Papal See, and some of the friars even insisted that the present incumbent was none other than the Antichrist himself, so the Bull was not entirely unreasonable in the circumstances. But William evidently thought it was. His reply, the *Opus Nonaginta Dierum* written in about 1332, went to great lengths to show that the papacy was not only corrupt, a state of affairs which was hardly news to his readers, but also heretical. In his list of past pontiffs who had not been 'pure, clean and saintly', he includes 'the woman who was venerated as pope', with no indication at all that he regards her as less real than the others, for 'it is held in the chronicles that she was revered as pope by the universal church for two years, seven months and three days.'[31]

Similar, but more extreme, anti-papal sentiments were expressed by the Bohemian reformer, John Hus, the former Rector of Prague University. He made use of Joan, under the name 'Agnes', in the course of his evidence at the Council of Constance, which was convened by the Pisan antipope, John XXIII, in 1414–15. Hus' argument was that the only true head of the Catholic Church was Christ himself, and that consequently the Church was quite capable of functioning without a terrestrial head during those periods when a corrupt or false pontiff, not predestined by God, was seated on the papal throne. It was for this reason, he explained, that the Church had been able to survive even though its members had been 'deceiv'd in the Person of Agnes' among others. The testimony, with its clear implication that all bad popes, including his contemporaries, could and should be deposed, was not exactly guaranteed to make Hus popular with the authorities. He was eventually condemned as a heretic by the Council and burned to death in 1415, despite the Imperial safe conduct given to him before he travelled to Constance.

In view of the Council members' attitude to Hus, it seems quite certain that they would have scoffed at his references to 'Agnes' if they had been at all doubtful about her reality. In the words of the eighteenth century historian, James L'Enfant: 'if it had not been looked upon at that Time as undeniable Fact, the Fathers of the Council wou'd not have fail'd either to correct John Hus with some Displeasure, and to have laugh'd and shook their Heads, as . . . they did presently for less Cause.'[32]

Thus was the woman pontiff's existence accepted.

3

DID JOAN EXIST?

SO FAR we have looked at the development and growth of Pope Joan's story during the Middle Ages, without actually stopping to ask how much, if any, of it was based on truth. Did a female pope ever hold sway over Rome, and if so, at what period did her reign take place? In order to answer these questions we must examine the situation in Rome around the middle of the ninth century and at the end of the eleventh: the alternative dates given for her by the medieval chroniclers.

It may well be thought that the Catholic Church has every reason to draw a veil over some of the curious events which occurred in ninth century Rome. There was, for instance, the strange trial of Pope Formosus, who died of natural causes in 896 after a pontificate of four and a half years. His remains were left in peace for only nine months, after which they were exhumed and dressed in papal vestments. The people of the city were then treated to the remarkable spectacle of a trial in which the defendant, charged with unlawful usurpation of the papal throne, was a decaying corpse. The affair was, of course, more for the benefit of the incumbent pope, Stephen VII, than for the humiliation of his predecessor who was presumably a little too far gone to care. Formosus was duly and predictably found guilty, and his body disposed of in the Tiber, from where it was later recovered, and finally interred in St Peter's Basilica by Pope Theodore II, during his twenty-day reign at the end of 897. Stephen VII himself profited nothing by the trial. He was thrown into prison shortly afterwards, and eventually strangled there. The details of the proceedings, which he had placed in the Lateran archives, were destroyed by the supporters of Formosus, but it is significant that even this powerful body of people was quite unable to remove all knowledge of the trial from the historical record. Modern authors, who suggest that there was a highly successful campaign to delete every reference to Pope Joan from all the documents written in the centuries following her death, may care to ponder upon this point.

In the sort of climate where dead popes could be exhumed for political reasons and living popes could be summarily despatched (at least six were killed while in office during the last half of the ninth century and the first half of the tenth),

5. Pope Leo IV. From Hartmannus Schedel's *Liber Chronicarum* (1493).

it would not be particularly surprising to find a woman on the throne of St Peter, between Leo IV and Benedict III. But if there was such a woman it should be easy to find some evidence of her, for the history of the papacy at this time is tolerably well documented, with a number of reliable contemporary sources and verbatim copies available for study.

It is known that the saintly Leo IV died on 17 July 855, and that on 29 September of the same year Benedict III was consecrated as his successor. Only a few days later, on 7 October (the nones of October), the new pontiff sent a decretal to the Monastery of Corbie, confirming its privileges.[1] This leaves a gap of some two and a half months, and on the face of it there is no room for the two years or more that Joan is said to have spent as pope. However, the situation is not entirely clear-cut.

On the death of Leo there were two main candidates for nomination as his replacement. One of these was Benedict himself, and the other was Anastasius, whom we have already encountered as the author of the *Liber Pontificalis*. It was Anastasius who had the vital support of the ailing Emperor Lothair and his son Louis II. Thus when a group of Roman nobles put forward Benedict instead, their choice did not receive Imperial ratification and Anastasius was able to impose himself on the papal seat for a few weeks, as a result of which he is nowadays recorded by the Catholic Church as an antipope.

Some eighteen months before Leo died, Anastasius had provoked his wrath by the way in which he was neglecting his duties as Priest of S. Marcello, a position to which Leo had appointed him in 847-8. Anastasius was anathematized in December 853,[2] and Leo caused a fresco to be put up in St Peter's to mark the event. Naturally, once on the papal throne, the antipope used his authority to have the annoying fresco destroyed. This action, together with his imprisonment of Benedict, hardly endeared him to the clergy of Rome, and in the face of growing hostility, the Imperial envoy prudently decided to withdraw his official support. Anastasius was then quickly overthrown in favour of Benedict.[3]

Despite the obvious differences between their respective reigns, is it possible that Anastasius might have been Pope Joan? He certainly ruled, albeit briefly, at the correct time, but there is little else to be said in favour of the idea, even if we disregard the female pope's pregnancy as a later fiction. We know that after losing the struggle with Benedict for the papacy, he became Abbot of the monastery of S. Maria in Trastavere. Later, as cardinal secretary and papal librarian, he wielded a great deal of political influence under Nicholas I (858-67) and Hadrian II (867-72). He was implicated in the kidnapping and murder of some of Pope Hadrian's relatives, but survived his trial for that offence and characteristically bounced back from disgrace into power. If the resilient Anastasius had been revealed as a woman during his days as an antipope, it is surely inconceivable that he could have gone on to enjoy such a long and illustrious career within the Church. Had there been even the slightest rumour about his sex, the issue would undoubtedly have been raised during his trial, so it is perfectly safe to rule out any connection between this unusual man and Pope Joan.

By the end of September 855, Anastasius was no longer a threat and the consecration of Benedict III duly went ahead on 29 September. A few days previously the Emperor Lothair, knowing himself to be gravely ill, had renounced his position in favour of his sons, Louis and Charles, and retired to the monastery at Prum in the Ardennes. He died there within hours of Benedict's inauguration, but news of his decease took some weeks to reach Rome, and during this period the first two *denarii* of the new pontiff's reign were minted. They both bore the names of 'Benedict Papa' and St Peter on one side, with 'Hlotharius Imp. Pius' on the reverse.[4] Subsequent issues, of course, replaced Lothair's name with that of Louis, but it is the existence of the two early coins, together with the Corbie decretal, which provides the final and irrefutable proof that Benedict could not have ascended to the papacy any later than the year 855.

Further evidence that no Pope John ruled between Leo IV and Benedict III appears in contemporary and near-contemporary documents, including correspondence between the main officials of Church and State. In a letter to Pope Nicholas I (858-67), for instance, the controversial Archbishop Hincmar of Rheims describes how, in 855, he sent his representatives to Rome with church documents addressed to Leo IV. On the road they were met by messengers bringing the news of Leo's death, and when they reached Rome they found a new pope occupying St Peter's throne. It was Benedict III.[5] Even the most scenic route to the city can hardly have taken the deputation more than two years to traverse, so there is no possibility of squeezing the reign of the female pope in here.

Nicholas I himself mentions 'my predecessors, Leo and Benedict of Blessed Memory' in a number of letters; and in a communication with the bishops of the Third Synod of Soissons, held in 866, he says: 'Pope Leo of the Apostolic See, who had been familiar with Brother Hincmar's purpose, died; and Benedict of Blessed Memory succeeded him.'[6] Similarly, the chronicle of Ado, Bishop of Vienna, which was written some time between 867 and 872, details the papal succession without a word about Pope Joan: 'The Roman Pontiff Gregory died, and in his place Sergius was appointed. When he died, Leo succeeded: on whose death Benedict was put in his place in the Apostolic See.'[7]

But perhaps Nicholas I and his bishops had good cause to remain quiet about such an embarrassing interlude in the history of the Church of Rome. The same cannot be said of Photius, who was made Patriarch of Constantinople in 858 and deposed seven years later, after an enquiry by Nicholas I into his election. Photius had every reason to dislike the Western Church, or at least its central establishment in Rome, and if the story of the woman pontiff had been known at that time, he would certainly have had no qualms at all about using it to show the papacy in a bad light. Yet in none of his works does he mention Pope Joan, and in one, where he lists the popes of his own era, he specifically describes 'Leo and Benedict, successively great priests of the Roman Church'.[8] The silence of someone like Photius, who had a grudge against Rome, is even more revealing than that of its supporters.

So all the evidence points in one direction: that no female pope could have reigned in the 850s. There is, however, another possibility to consider before we leave the ninth century altogether. According to several writers, from Tolomeo of Lucca in 1312 onwards, Pope Joan took the title 'John VIII' when she began her pontificate. Could the real John VIII then have been a woman? It seems highly unlikely. This John sat on the papal throne for ten years, from 872–82. He was a 'warrior pope' and a ruthless man with many equally ruthless enemies, including the ill-fated future pope Formosus, whose post-mortem clash with the ecclesiastical courts has already been mentioned. John died violently; he seems to have been beaten to death after an attempt to poison him had failed. His life bears no resemblance at all to that of Joan, and if John had been revealed as a woman, those who opposed him would not have needed to resort to such drastic means to remove him from power.

The alternative title of 'John VII', which a few authors preferred for the female pope, was probably the result of a miscalculation, as they all—with one exception—persist in placing her pontificate in the ninth century, even though the real John VII ruled far earlier than that: from 705–7. The exception is the copyist of Otto of Frisingen's chronicle, who added the word *foemina* after the name of the historical John VII. But as we saw in the first chapter, he did not produce his edition until the reign of Leo X (1513–21) at the earliest, and his mistake seems to have been due to the omission of all dates from Otto's papal catalogue. In truth, the Greek man who became John VII, and whose body was buried in St Peter's Basilica upon his perfectly natural death in 707, had but one thing in common with Pope Joan: he also ruled for two years and some months.

A letter which was sent in 1054 to Michael Cerularius, Patriarch of Constantinople, from the Supreme Pontiff Leo IX (1049–54), proves conclusively that the story of the female pope had not yet arisen, or at least that it was still unknown in Rome even though the main events were supposed to have taken place there. This document is important for other reasons and will be discussed fully in the next chapter.

Since we are forced to accept that there is no place for Pope Joan in the ninth century, then what of the eleventh? The earliest sources which we have discovered locate her at the very end of that century, and logically this older tradition should be the more authentic, especially as the gap between her rule and its first chroniclers would thus be only about 150 years. Jean de Mailly, writing around 1250 in his *Chronica Universalis*, states that there was a woman pope in 1099. His compatriot, Stephen of Bourbon, places her at approximately 1100 even though he copies most of his other details directly from Jean de Mailly, whom he acknowledges by name in the course of his treatise. Such a minor disagreement indicates a certain vagueness on the part of the authors, but it is not of any significance. Nevertheless, we would be well advised not to confine ourselves strictly to those two years when searching for a female pontiff at this time.

A significant feature of the years around 1100 was the number of antipopes who appeared in quick succession on the ecclesiastical stage. Their unusual profusion was due to power struggles between a variety of factions both inside and outside the Church, and in particular to the intervention of the Emperor Henry IV (1056–1106) throughout the period. The famous Pope Gregory VII, who had the knack of making influential enemies on several fronts at once, died in 1085 and by the end of his rule he had lost the support of almost all the Roman clergy. They had, in the main, given their allegiance to the Emperor's antipope, Clement III. In the year 1084, Rome was occupied by Henry's army, and Henry had himself crowned as Emperor by Clement. Gregory meanwhile was under siege in the papal fortress of Castel Sant'Angelo. He appealed for help to the Normans, but they proved to be a bad choice as, by the time they arrived, Henry had already retreated northwards, and the Normans contented themselves with sacking the city. They then returned to Sicily, taking Gregory with them. He died at Salerno on 25 May, 1085, and for exactly a year there was no official pontiff in Rome, although Clement III continued in his unofficial position.

On 24 May, 1086, Victor III reluctantly assumed the papal throne, but he lived for less than a year and a half, after which there was an interregnum of only six months before he was succeeded by Odo, Bishop of Ostia, who took the name Urban II. Clement was still in Rome, and the Emperor controlled a great deal of Italy, so Urban's installation as pope took place in Terracina, one hundred kilometres south-east of the city. He was unable to establish his presence in Rome until 1097, although he had in the meantime secured a prominent place for himself in medieval history by proclaiming the First Crusade from the steps of the Cathedral at Clermont-Ferrand.

Just two weeks after the death of Urban at the end of July 1099, the new pope, Paschal II, was consecrated, but it was some time before his authority became undisputed. In addition to Clement III (1080–1100), the antipopes Theodoric (1100–2), Albert (1102) and Sylvester IV (1105–11) all enjoyed the support of one faction or another within Rome, and as a result gained a brief ascendancy to the discomfiture of Paschal. Even so he survived them all, and his reign of nearly nineteen years was the longest since Leo III (795–816). The contention of Jean de Mailly that Paschal II did not ascend the throne of St Peter until 1106, thus leaving room for Pope Joan, collapses in the face of the established facts.

If the two early chroniclers had a particular reason for placing the story of the female pontiff in the years around 1100, then no doubt it had something to do with the confusion of popes and antipopes which existed at the time. It is too great a leap of logic, however, to assume that one of these rival popes was a woman in disguise. There are no similarities between their lives and that of our subject to justify us in doing so.

We may have been completely unsuccessful in our attempts to find Pope Joan, but the lack of contemporary, written evidence does not in itself rule out the possibility of her existence. After all, references to Jesus Christ only started to appear some two decades after his supposed crucifixion, and even then the Christ whom we encounter in St Paul's letters is in no way a fleshed-out human being. When the first of the Gospels, that of St Mark, was compiled, Jesus had been dead for forty years. Yet most people, rightly or wrongly, accept him as a historical figure. A minor first century religious leader, though, is rather more easily missed by his contemporaries than a ninth or eleventh century Supreme Pontiff of the Western Church. The great problem in the case of the female pope is that the papal lists for the times when she is said to have ruled contain no suspicious or unexplained gaps, into which she might be fitted. On the contrary there is a considerable amount of positive evidence proving that other well-authenticated popes reigned throughout both periods.

Before coming to any firm conclusions about the reality or otherwise of Pope Joan, there are four matters associated with her story which need to be looked at more closely. They include the avoidance of a certain street by the popes when in procession, a memorial inscription, a statue of a mother and child, and a pierced seat used in papal ceremonial.

(1) The Shunned Street

The Lateran Palace came into the hands of the Church in the fourth century as a gift from the Emperor Constantine. It had previously been an imperial palace, but immediately became the main residence of the Pope in Rome. The basilica which Constantine raised alongside, on the site of a cavalry barracks, was regarded as the episcopal cathedral of the Pope as Bishop of Rome. Now largely reconstructed in the Baroque style, St John Lateran continues to serve the same purpose today. The Lateran is on the opposite side of Rome to the other main focus of papal activity, the Vatican and St Peter's; and so throughout the Middle Ages, whenever a pope was resident in the city, there was a frequent passing and re-passing of pontifical processions from the one location to the other. The route between them includes both the Colosseum and the great Basilica of St Clement, built on the site of a third century Mithraeum. These two ancient buildings are linked by the Via S. Giovanni in Laterano, but in the later Middle Ages this direct road— which, it appears, contained some kind of statue—was avoided, supposedly out of abhorrence of Pope Joan who was believed to have given birth and died there while on her way from St Peter's.

We know for certain that the detour was made almost as a matter of course during the fifteenth century. In 1486, John Burchard, Bishop of Strasbourg and papal Master of Ceremonies under Innocent VIII (1484–92), Alexander VI (1492–1503), Pius III (1503) and Julius II (1503–13), organized a procession for

6. Pope Joan in childbirth. From Giovanni Boccaccio's *De Mulieribus Claris* (1539 Berne edition).

Innocent VIII which broke with tradition by passing along the shunned street. His *Liber Notarum* records the heavy criticism to which he was subjected as a result:

In going as in returning, he (the pope) came by way of the Colisseum, and that straight road where the statue of the female pope (*imago papissae*) is located, in token, it is said, that John VII Anglicus gave birth there to a child. For that reason, many say the popes are never allowed to ride on horseback there. Therefore the Lord Archbishop of Florence, the Bishop of Massano, and Hugo de Bencii the Apostolic Subdeacon, delivered a reprimand to me. However, I had words on this subject with the Lord Bishop of Pienza, who told me that it is foolishness and heresy to think that the popes are prohibited from travelling by this street, no authentic document or custom being known which would prevent them.[9]

Although Burchard seems to have doubted the link between the female pope's death and this particular stretch of road, it will be noticed that he was not necessarily questioning her existence as such. His concern was more with challenging the necessity of protecting the reigning pontiff from a sight of the image of his notorious predecessor.

The standard and oft-repeated modern explanation for the diversion away from the most direct route, is that the roadway at this point was too narrow for a procession to pass in comfort, at least until the rebuilding and road-widening works carried out by Sixtus V (1585–90) improved the situation. If this were so, Burchard would surely have remarked on the fact, whereas in reality his procession appears to have found no difficulty at all in using the street.

The true solution to the mystery probably lies in the fact that there were no popes in Rome between 1308 and 1367, and indeed the curia did not officially return from Avignon until 1377. Thus it was that at the precise time when Pope Joan's story, as given by the interpolator of Martin Polonus, was becoming popular, there was no possibility of verifying his claims concerning the papal detour. We only have his word, and that of those authors who copied from him, for its existence prior to the Avignon Captivity. Certainly no one before Martin makes any mention of the diversion, let alone specifying the point at which it occurred. It seems likely that Martin's copyist invented the whole idea, perhaps to add further spice (if such were needed) or verisimilitude to his tale. Thereafter it was picked and repeated so many times that when the popes returned to the city they adopted the practice on the assumption that it was a genuine tradition, little realizing its recent origins.

Hypothesis this may be but it accords with all the available information, which is more than can be said for the assertion that the female pontiff met her end in the shunned street, or that the road there was simply too narrow for processions.

(2) The Memorial Stone

The two earliest accounts of Pope Joan, which date from the middle of the thirteenth century, refer to this memorial stone with its alliterative inscription, while three other writers place the words from the stone into the mouth of a demon. There is some disagreement among these sources, however, on the exact details of the wording, all of the following being given as alternatives: *Petre Pater Patrum, Papisse Prodito Partum* (Jean de Mailly); *Parce, Pater Patrum, Papisse Prodere Partum* (Stephen of Bourbon); and *Papa, Pater Patrum, Papiss(a)e Pandito Partum* (*Chronica Minor, Flores Temporum* and, somewhat later, Theodoric Engelhusius).

If the stone ever existed, and it is quite possible that it did, then we have no way of knowing where it was located. The authors who mention it say no more than that the memorial was set up at the place where the woman pontiff died. Stephen of Bourbon alone adds that it was 'outside the city'. Her death, according to this version of events, was the result of a standard form of Roman execution, and it happened at a point at least half a league distant from her confinement. Neither of the two dramas was in any way associated with the street between St Clement's Church and the Colosseum, which became a part of the story only after the *Chronicon* of Martin Polonus started to circulate some thirty years later.

The stone has long since disappeared, no doubt lost during restoration work or street-widening operations. Nevertheless the origin of the inscription is not difficult to trace, for many others which resemble it are recorded in J.C. Von Orelli's *Inscriptionum Latinarum*. The lack of consensus on the exact wording suggests that the final three words at least were either partially illegible or represented simply by their initial letters, 'P.P.P.' In Classical Rome such abbreviations were very common on memorial stones. Von Orelli lists one which features no less than five consecutive initials, 'V.P.P.P.R.', probably for *Vice-Praefectus Praetorio Provinciae Raetiarum*.[10] 'P.P.P.' can be interpreted in several ways, but by far the most likely in the context we are considering is *Pecunia Propria Posuit* or '(he) placed this with his own money'.

The first word of the inscription, variously given in the sources as *Petre, Parce* and *Papa*, is too diversely described to be identified today, although it was doubtless the name of the person who paid for the memorial, perhaps shortened to *Pap.* or *Pet.* The one thing on which all the chroniclers agree is the phrase *Pater Patrum* (Father of Fathers); in actuality a title of some antiquity. Nearly 2000 years ago a large number of Roman men, especially within the army and imperial service, were worshippers of Mithras. Members of the cult passed through seven degrees of initiation: Raven, Occult, Soldier, Lion, Persian, Runner of the Sun and finally Father (*Pater*). The most distinguished priests of the order, at the summit of the seventh degree, were styled *Pater Patrum*, and Von Orelli quotes several examples from memorials which either include the straightforward *Pater Patrum* or elaborate it to *Pater Patrum Dei Solis Invicti Mithrae* (Father of

Fathers of the Invincible Sun God Mithras).[11]

Thus we can be reasonably certain that Pope Joan's monument, if it did indeed exist, was actually erected by an important Mithraic priest of the second or third century AD, many hundreds of years before Joan is said to have lived.

This type of misinterpretation or deliberate misreading of a Classical inscription has occurred in Rome on more than one occasion. Around AD150, for instance, Justin Martyr stated that the notorious magician Simon Magus had preached and been worshipped in Rome some time during the previous century, and as proof of this he adduced a Roman statue which he had heard about, but not personally seen. This figure, he said, was dedicated 'To Simon, the Holy God' (*Simoni Deo Sancto*). Unfortunately the likelihood is that Justin was fooled by a representation of the old Sabine god Semo Sancus, who was commemorated with the not dissimilar phrase *Semoni Sanco Deo Fidio* on a stone re-discovered in the sixteenth century. There is no other evidence that Simon Magus ever even visited Rome, although the idea was taken up with enthusiasm by the writer of the *Golden Legend* among others.

Such myths have often arisen out of attempts to understand obscure inscriptions, with the application of large doses of wishful thinking and imagination. This fact has led some modern authors to the rather implausible conclusion that the entire history of Pope Joan was devised in an effort to make sense of the seemingly incomprehensible *Pater Patrum* memorial. They mistakenly assume that it was connected with, or perhaps even on the pedestal of, the Roman statue of the woman pontiff which was recorded by various writers from 1375 onwards. However, the inscription is never mentioned by these later witnesses, and there can be little doubt that it was a completely separate and unrelated object, probably even situated in another part of the city altogether. Since it was ignored by Martin Polonus' interpolator, and by all the chroniclers who followed him, the stone can never have been widely associated with the female pope, and any central role for it in the genesis of her story can be ruled out.

(3) The Statue

While the reality of the inscribed stone must remain uncertain, there is no such problem with the statue, believed to represent Pope Joan and her child, which stood somewhere in the narrow street between the Colosseum and St Clement's Basilica. On its exact position the old writers do not quite agree. Some, like the *Mirabilia Urbis Romae*, say that it was 'nigh unto the Colosseum', but others accord more closely with Adam of Usk's description of it as 'near St Clement's'. If Adam was correct then the object may have been located at the point by St Clement's where the road towards the Church of SS Quattro Incoronati branches from the Via S. Giovanni in Laterano. Alternatively it might have been much closer to the Colosseum, perhaps right at that end of the street. In Lafrery's map of 1557 a small building is drawn at the appropriate spot between the ends of the Via S. Giovanni and the Via Labicana. Possibly the figure was within a niche in one of its exterior walls. It is worth noting, in this connection, that a few late authors refer to a 'House of Pope Joan' near the statue. However, there would seem to be some confusion here with the 'House of Pope John' (domus Iohannis papae), which was recorded in the area between the Colosseum and St Clement's as early as the twelfth century, and which had no connection with the woman pontiff.

After the statue's first appearance in the Mirabilia of around 1375, it was mentioned by many commentators including, as we have seen, the papal Master of Ceremonies, John Burchard, in 1486. When Martin Luther visited Rome, probably late in the year 1510, he also remarked upon it and expressed his surprise that the popes should allow so embarrassing an object to remain in a public place. The image which Luther saw was that of a woman wearing a papal cloak, and holding a child and a sceptre.[12] Vague as this is it is actually the best description available to us. No other writer gives as much detail and, indeed, only one or two go so far as to note that the main figure was accompanied by a baby or child.

This lack of contemporary data makes it impossible for us to come to any definite conclusions as to the nature of the statue, which was removed in the latter half of the sixteenth century, perhaps during renovation work under Sixtus V (1585–90). It could have been an image of Pope Joan exactly as claimed, and in that case it must have been erected on the traditional site of her death some time around the middle of the fourteenth century, when her story was beginning to be widely accepted as true. This would tie in well with the fact that the statue seems to have been completely unknown until about 1375, but not so well with Theodoric of Niem's statement that it was 'erected by Pope Benedict (III), in order to inspire a horror of the scandal which took place on that spot'.[13] Theodoric was writing around 1414 and, if the figure was little more than fifty years old at the time, he would surely not have made such a mistake in dating it. There is another, perhaps more likely, explanation. A pre-existing carving of a mother and her child, probably from the Classical period, could have come to be connected with the female pope for no other reason than it happened to stand in or near the street which Martin Polonus' interpolator associated with her downfall. It is vital to remember that rumours about the avoidance of this street by the popes began to appear nearly one hundred years before the stone image became a part of the standard story.

If the statue was of a Classical date then the theory set out by G. Tomassetti in his article, 'La Statua Della Papessa Giovanna',[14] looks extremely promising. He believes that a certain figure which still survives in the Chiaramonti Gallery of the Vatican Museum is the very one which we have been discussing. It is a charming portrayal of a serene and dignified young woman suckling a child.

She is heavily and modestly robed and wears a diadem upon her head, while the baby which she holds on her lap is quite naked. Such groupings were surprisingly rare in ancient Rome. According to Tomassetti the only other one to have survived is of Ino suckling Bacchus, a rather less decorous depiction of motherhood, which was formerly in the courtyard of the Lante Palace.

The sculpture now in the Vatican probably represents Juno suckling the infant Heracles, as she was supposedly tricked into doing in order to ensure his immortality. Or perhaps it is an abstract personification of fertility, although this seems less likely. If it is to be identified, however tentatively, with the famous image of Pope Joan, then obviously a link must be established between it and the shunned street. Tomassetti's efforts to prove the existence of such a link depend upon the premise that Joan's statue was removed by Sixtus V. It is known that the present Vatican figure came from the Quirinal Gardens, which were created by Sixtus in the late 1580s, and decorated with ancient marbles. These he obtained readily enough from various areas of Rome during a massive re-building programme, which he undertook throughout the city. It was at this time that he widened and improved the narrow street between St Clement's and the Colosseum. The financial accounts of the establishment of the Quirinal Gardens survive, but unfortunately the transport of the marbles was sub-contracted, and is recorded only as a lump sum without itemization. Thus there is no way of telling whether any of the works of art were taken from that particular roadway. Without such a vital piece of evidence the identification of the female pope's statue with the Classical sculpture from the Quirinal can only be considered as an attractive but unproven possibility.

Moreover it poses its own set of problems, which Tomassetti ignores. Where, for instance, is the sceptre which Martin Luther saw in 1510? The existing figure carries nothing apart from the baby, and although Tomassetti points out that the woman's shoulder and right arm have been restored, it seems aesthetically unlikely that she could ever have held any additional object. The proposed date of the old statue's disappearance is not entirely borne out by other sources either. St Robert Bellarmine (1542–1621), the celebrated Jesuit cardinal, composed his *De Summo Pontifice* in 1577, a few years before Sixtus V ascended the papal throne. Yet in its pages he persistently refers to Pope Joan's image in the past tense, with the clear implication that it had already been pulled down. His description of it is remarkably odd too, for he maintains that it did not depict a woman with an infant on her lap at all. Instead, the larger figure was male and the smaller was 'a fairly large child, several years old, preceding like a servant'. [15] He therefore conjectures that the group was of 'some pagan priest prepared for a sacrifice and preceded by his attendant'. Meagre as the eye-witness accounts of the statue are, they cannot be made to accord with this. The obvious deduction is that Bellarmine never saw it for himself, and this being the case perhaps we should accept the testimony of Elias Hasenmuller who, in the last decade of the sixteenth century, was told on good authority that the image had been thrown into the Tiber by Pius V (1566–72).[16]

But what are we to make of the statue of Pope Joan which the Englishman Thomas Harding saw some time prior to 1565, 'graven in a stone, after the manner of a tombstone, pitched upright not far from the Colosseo'?[17] This object, he declared, no more resembled a figure than do the rough-hewn stones at Stonehenge and Great Rollright or the natural rock formation known as the Witch of Wookey Hole.

In truth, we can be sure of almost nothing concerning the statue apart from the bare fact that it existed, and was closely connected with the female pontiff for at least 150 years.

(4) The Pierced Seat

The consecration of each new pope took place in the Basilica of St John Lateran, the papal cathedral. For approximately four centuries, during the late Middle Ages, not just one but two pierced seats were used in the ceremony. They were known as the *sedia curules*, a phrase which in ancient Rome denoted the thrones on which the Consuls sat. At a certain point in the consecration service the new pontiff proceeded to the Chapel of St Sylvester where the chairs were situated, and sat first on one, then on the other, while a ritual was enacted. The exact nature of this ritual is revealed by papal Master of Ceremonies, John Burchard, in his detailed and reliable description of the coronation of Innocent VIII on 12 September, 1484:

. . . the pope was led to the door of St Sylvester's chapel, near which were placed two plain porphyry seats, in the first of which, from the right of the door, the pope sat, as though lying down: and when he was thus seated, the . . . prior of the Lateran gave into the pope's hand a rod in token of ruling and correction and the keys of the Basilica and the Lateran Palace, in token of the power of closing and opening, of binding and loosing.[18]

The pontiff then moved to the second chair in order to hand back the rod and keys.

No one, least of all the Church authorities, can reasonably question the existence of the seats, nor the fact that they were pierced, for one survives in Rome to this day. Pius VI had them both removed from St John's to the Vatican Museum in the late eighteenth century, and one still remains there, in the Museo Pio Clementino. The other found its way to Paris as part of the loot from Napoleon's invasion of Italy—loot which contained many works of art as well as a large part of the Vatican archives. Although the archives were eventually returned to Rome, the seat was not, and it is now in the Louvre Museum. Cesare D'Onofrio includes photographs of the two chairs in his *La Papessa Giovanna* (1979),[19] but when we enquired after the one in the Louvre we were told by a representative that the Museum '*ne conserve pas de trône pontifical.*' There are some who will choose to see this as yet another manifestation of a long-running conspiracy to hide and obscure the truth of the Pope Joan story!

To judge from D'Onofrio's pictures, the chairs have survived the passage of time very well. They are still handsome objects; both carved in red marble and practically identical in design. It is said that they were discovered in an old Roman bath and, whether or not this is true, there is no doubt that they date back to Classical times. Presumably they were used in the consecration purely because of their undeniably impressive appearance, for the holes in their seats would seem to have been irrelevant to the ceremonial itself. They may originally have been made as commodes, but D'Onofrio has argued in favour of a different explanation for their perforation. He asserts that the thrones were intended as obstetric chairs; indeed this is quite a tenable theory in view of their close resemblance to others, such as one in blue stone in the British Museum, which served that purpose. D'Onofrio goes one step further and speculates that they wee used by the Catholic authorities to symbolize the position of St John Lateran as the Mother Church. Undoubtedly this distinction was claimed, and from the twelfth century it was emphasized by an inscription, *Mater et Caput Omnium Ecclesiarum* (Mother and Head of All the Churches), which was carved on the Cathedral's façade. However, the connection between this title and the pierced seats is not convincing. Using the principles of Occam's Razor, there is no need to look any further than their obvious beauty and splendour to explain their employment in the papal consecration.

As we have already seen, it was commonly reported during the late Middle Ages that the seats were perforated so that a deacon could check the sex of the newly-appointed pope and make sure that he was not a eunuch or a woman in disguise. Nevertheless, there was no shortage of contemporary writers who cast doubts on these rumours. One thing which contributed to the general confusion and disagreement was the existence of a third chair, which was not one of the *sedia curules*. This *sedes stercoraria* also played a part in the enthronement ritual. In 1479 the Prefect of the Vatican Library, Bartolomeo Platina, referred to it when discounting the popular story:

(This) . . . we feel arises from the seat having been equipped in order that the person enthroned should know themselves not divine but human, and subject to the necessities of nature, whereby the seat is called the *sedes stercoraria*.[20]

This third chair was of white marble, placed at the entrance to the Basilica, and—contrary to Platina's hints—it was not pierced like the others. It never left St John Lateran and remains there, though rather the worse for wear, to this day. The name given to it derives solely from its use at a certain point in the ceremony, when the words *Suscitat de pulvere egenum et de stercore erigit pauperem, ut sedeat cum principibus et solium glorie teneat* were chanted while the new pope reclined upon it. The quotation, 'He raises up the poor out of the dust and lifts the needy out of the dunghill; That he may sit with princes and hold the throne with glory' (Psalm 113: 7–8), was supposed to remind the pontiff that he was but a humble man, despite his exalted status.

Afterwards, before leaving the white chair, the pope was given three handfuls of coins, which he threw to the people, saying 'Gold and silver are not mine, but that which I have I give to you.'[21]

It is easy to understand how the confusion between the three seats could have arisen among those who were not intimately involved with the workings of the Lateran. Having heard about one or more pierced chairs, they would naturally have assumed that the *sedes stercoraria* or 'dung seat' was the most likely candidate. They little realized that its title implied nothing about its nature. Even Vatican officials like Platina were capable of making this error, and the misunderstanding has had a very long life. Some modern guidebooks to Rome still persist in repeating it.[22]

All three thrones were first mentioned in descriptions of the consecration of Pope Paschal II in August, 1099. Strangely enough, Jean de Mailly and Stephen of Bourbon both chose to place the ascendancy of Pope Joan at around 1099 or 1100, but it is hard to see how this coincidence of dates can be anything more than chance, curious though it is. Tales of the sexing of the pope had not yet started to appear when they were writing, and neither author remarks on the new ritual in the context of the woman pontiff, or anywhere else for that matter.

The chairs played their part in subsequent ceremonies for several hundred years, ending with the reign of Leo X, whose enthronement in 1513 was the last to feature them. His successor, the saintly Hadrian VI (1522–3), abolished their use in the course of his reforms. Perhaps his decision was prompted by the foolish and unpleasant rumours about them, which were at the height of their popularity by then, and showed no signs of fading.

The story of the examination of each new pope to prove that he was really a man was certainly a favourite one, but it was undoubtedly pure invention. In the official sources throughout the period, such as the *Ordo Romanus* which contains the directions for the consecration ceremonial, it is conspicuous only by its absence. And witnesses to events in Rome well before the time of John Burchard call the tale a 'senseless popular fable', to use the words of Jacobo d'Agnola di Scarperia, written after the inauguration of Gregory XII in 1406.[23]

However, juicy scandal of this sort takes a long time to lose its appeal. The fact that the chairs ceased to fulfil even their completely innocent function after 1513 did not deter later writers, like the Swede Lawrence Banck, from claiming that the pope's sex was still being ascertained in the 'traditional' manner. In Banck's case, the enthronement in question was that of Innocent X in 1644.

It is hardly surprising, therefore, that Pius VI took the final step of removing the pierced seats from the Lateran in the following century.

We have explored all the avenues of enquiry which might have led us to a historical female pontiff, and on investigation the evidence has come to very little. It has also been quite impossible to find any suspicious lacunae in the papal lists for the appropriate periods. The obvious conclusion, albeit a reluctant one, must be that the legend of Pope Joan is just that and nothing more.

4

FACTS AND THEORIES

HOW and when did the story of Pope Joan arise, and was it a deliberate fabrication? If so, to what purpose? These are the obvious questions which remain to be answered if the woman pontiff did not actually exist.

The statue and the pierced seats can have little bearing on the problem since they only became widely linked with the tale one hundred years or more after its inception, and long after it had gained great popularity in its own right. Cesare D'Onofrio's claim that the story grew from a symbolic act of childbirth by each new pope (representing the Mother Church), while seated on the pierced chairs, can be dismissed for the same reason. His supposition that 'the father assumed the position of labour'[1] during the ceremony of the handing over of the keys is intriguing, especially in view of John Burchard's use of the phrase 'as though lying down' in this context, but it is not relevant to Pope Joan.

There are many other theories to choose from, but a number make the unnecessary and false assumption that a mysterious event in the ninth century must have provoked the legend. These can be discounted by some of the same arguments as we have advanced for the rejection of Pope Joan herself: in particular the lack of contemporary sources and the fact that the myth did not appear until four hundred years later. A representative example is the belief of Professor N.C. Kist,[2] in the last century, that the female pope was the widow of her predecessor, Leo IV, and ruled in conjunction with his successor Benedict III. Thus did Kist ingeniously fit her in where there was in reality no room.

The basic idea that a married man could become the supreme pontiff is not in the least unreasonable. Only a few years after Leo IV, the septuagenarian Hadrian II (867–72) actually had his wife and daughter living with him in the Lateran Palace, until they were kidnapped and then killed by Eleutherius, a relative of Anastasius the Librarian. At that time the Fourth Lateran Council and the enforcement of clerical celibacy were more than 300 years in the future. In the case of Leo, though, there is not a shred of evidence to suggest that he ever married, and Kist's remarkable hypothesis is not even hinted at in any of the medieval chronicles.

Cardinal Baronius, the Vatican librarian at the beginning of the seventeenth century, thought that the real John VIII (872–82) might have been maliciously called a 'woman' because of his supposedly 'easy and pliable nature',[3] particularly in connection with his re-instatement of Photius as Patriarch of Constantinople. This view does not stand up if we examine the known facts about John, who was a ruthless opportunist and an aggressive personality to say the least. A similar theory concerning John VII (705–7) was put forward shortly after Baronius' time, but it would seem to be equally ill-founded. John VII is said to have been jeered at as a 'woman' for his lack of vigour in proscribing the canons of the Council of Trullo (692), which had been emphatically rejected by his predecessor, Sergius I.

Other suggestions about the legend can be discarded just as speedily. The prolific late-Victorian author, Sabine Baring-Gould, was a man of many quaint notions, some of which are revealed in his *Curious Myths of the Middle Ages*. On the female pontiff, he has this to say:

I have little doubt myself that Pope Joan is an impersonification of the great whore of Revelation, seated on the seven hills, and is the popular expression of the idea prevalent from the twelfth to the sixteenth centuries, that the mystery of iniquity was somehow working in the papal court. The scandal of the Antipopes, the utter worldliness and pride of others . . . along with the words of Revelation prophesying the advent of an adulterous woman who should rule over the imperial city, and her connexion with Antichrist, crystallized into this curious myth.[4]

There is a certain appeal to the thought, and it seems to be quite true that a few authors did equate Joan with the Scarlet Woman of Revelation. Petrarch, for one, was surely hinting at such a thing when he listed the horrors which followed her reign. Nevertheless, the tale was current for a long time before it started to take on such symbolic overtones, and they cannot have been involved in its beginnings. That the papacy was often, and from an early date, identified with the Great Whore of the Apocalypse in the polemic of its enemies is undeniable, but the image was considered as referring to the Bishops of Rome in general rather than to any specific one.

At first sight, a more acceptable theory is that which is advanced in the *Encyclopaedia Britannica* and in the part-work *The Unexplained*[5] among other places, tracing the origin of the female pope to the House of Theophylact. The Theophylact in question was a tenth-century Roman senator whose wife, Theodora, had a friend and supposed lover in Ravenna, where he held an ecclesiastical office. Under her protection he became the Bishop of Ravenna and then, in 914, ascended the papal throne as John X. Theodora died in about 924, and in a coup which her daughter Marozia organized some four years later, John X was imprisoned in Castel Sant'Angelo where he soon died in suspicious circumstances. His successors, Leo VI and Stephen VIII were also quickly murdered, and in 931 John XI took office. This young man was the son of Marozia, and rumour had it that his father was Pope Sergius III, who ruled from 904–11.

The new pontiff's position depended entirely on the continuing authority of his mother, but when she made an unpopular marriage in 933 her other son, Alberic, took advantage of the situation and ousted her from power. She died, or was killed, shortly afterwards. John XI meanwhile was allowed to remain on the papal throne for just as long as it served his half-brother's purposes. In 935 he was deposed and Alberic, now in full temporal control of Rome, made sure that the succession of popes who followed were little more than his puppets. Eventually, a year or two after Alberic's death, his own son Octavius became supreme pontiff in 955, adopting the title of John XII. It was soon clear that this John had little regard for the religious implications of his office, and he became notorious for his immorality, even in that turbulent age. He had a number of mistresses whom he endowed with riches from the coffers of the Church, and one particular favourite he even set up as a feudal lord.

During his reign, John was faced with the military threat of King Berengar of Italy, and he called on Otto, King of the Saxons, to render assistance. Otto did as he was requested, but then took the Papal States as part of his own domain; an outcome not at all to the liking of the Pope, who was forced to turn for aid to his former enemy, Berengar. Otto returned to Rome and deposed John in 963, on the grounds of his gross immorality. Five months later he was murdered, apparently while on the way to visit his mistress.

But the Theophylact story did not quite end there. The family regained influence in the early part of the next century and produced three more popes, the progeny of John's brother, Gregory. Benedict VIII (1012–24) and John XIX (1024–32) were both great-grandsons of Marozia, and Benedict IX (1032–48 with breaks) was her great-great-grandson.

Our main source of contemporary information on the tenth century Theophylacts is Liudprand of Cremona, the tone of whose account can be gathered from these introductory words:

A certain shameless strumpet called Theodora . . . at one time was sole monarch of Rome and—shame upon us even to say the words!—exercised power in the most manly fashion. She had two daughters, Marotia and Theodora, and these damsels were not only her equals but could even surpass her in the exercises that Venus loves.[6]

Liudprand had an axe to grind, being a supporter of Otto of Saxony and therefore an enemy not only of John XII but of all his forbears as well. Nevertheless it is clear that Marozia undertook a considerable amount of political machination, and was unscrupulous in her quest for power, though no more so than many a man of her time. People have always been only too willing to believe ill of ambitious women, and one cannot help but wonder whether Liudprand's biased statements would have been uncritically accepted for so long if he had been discussing a less female-dominated family. Modern opinion[7] has tended to redeem the Theophylacts from the black picture which the older writers liked to paint of them. Theodora the Elder seems to have been a much more faithful and pious person than Liudprand would have us believe, and no one has ever discovered any lapse on the part of Marozia's sister, the other Theodora, who was a blameless character so far as we know.

A number of authors have claimed that the legend of Pope Joan grew out of a confused memory of this period when puppet pontiffs acted under the direction of the Theophylact women, who constituted a 'power behind the throne' and could, perhaps with some justice in the case of Marozia, be maligned as 'female popes' in rather the same manner as Mrs Proudie was regarded as the Bishop of Barchester. But if this were truly the origin of the story, then why did it not arise within a short time of the era concerned, instead of more than 300 years later? And why, when it did eventually see the light of day, was it not set correctly in the tenth century by a single one of its many chroniclers?

There seems to be no way around these difficulties, and we believe that Pope Joan's origin has to be sought in a totally different direction. In fact we have already touched upon the letter which contains our first positive clue. It was written by Pope Leo IX to Michael Cerularius, the Patriarch of Constantinople, in 1054:

God forbid that we wish to believe what public opinion does not hesitate to claim has happened to the Church of Constantinople; namely that in promoting eunuchs indiscriminately against the First Law of the Council of Nicaea, it once raised a woman on to the seat of its pontiff. We regard this crime as so abominable and horrible that although outrage and horror of it and brotherly goodwill do not allow us to believe it; nevertheless, reflecting upon your carelessness towards the judgement of Holy Law, we consider that it could have happened because even now you indifferently and repeatedly promote eunuchs and those who are weak in some part of their body not only into clerical office, but also to the position of pontiff.[8]

This attack on the patriarchate is important for two reasons. To begin with it confirms, by implication, our conclusion that the tale of the female pope was unknown in the eleventh century. In 1054 the final schism between the Eastern and Western Churches occurred, and there was no love lost between their respective leaders. Leo IX would scarcely have risked raising the subject of a woman patriarch of Constantinople if he had been aware of a similar stain on the Church of Rome, a stain which Michael Cerularius would not have hesitated to throw straight back in his face if it had existed.

Even more interesting, and demanding of further investigation, is the information that rumours of another female religious leader were rife when the letter was sent. If there were no corroboration from other sources this could, no doubt, be dismissed as a fiction invented by Pope Leo in order to support his argument, but the evidence shows that the story to which he was referring dated back over 150 years. The *Chronicon Salernitanum*, of around 980, tells it thus:

At that time (during the reign of Charlemagne) a certain patriarch ruled over Constantinople, a good and just man but undoubtedly defiled by carnal love, so much so that he kept his niece in his house as though she were a eunuch, and wrapped her all around in beautiful apparel. This patriarch, when close to death, commended his nephew, as she seemed to be, to the favour of all. Upon his demise they all, being in complete ignorance, chose with one voice she who was a woman, as their bishop. She presided over them for almost a year and a half. But in the night time, when weary limbs are subdued by sleep, an evil spirit appeared before the bed where Arichis was sleeping, and it spoke aloud, proclaiming, 'What are you doing, Arichis?'. While he was making sense of the unusual clamour in his ears, the devil spoke again: 'I will disclose to you what I have done. The people of Constantinople have certainly elected a woman, and therefore it is engaging the wrath of the redeemer of that land.' And saying this he departed. At once the same prince sent envoys to Constantinople, and they ascertained that all which the devil had revealed to him was true, and then this abomination was put an end to.[9]

Erchempert, monk and poet of Monte Cassino, also mentions Arichis' dream and its consequences, in his history of the Lombards of Southern Italy, which was written as early as the last decade of the ninth century.[10] His version adds that after her overthrow the false patriarch was imprisoned in a nunnery, while the plague which God had unleashed on the city as punishment for her impropriety swiftly died out.

Although no precise date is given for these events, a fair approximation can be made. Prince Arichis, the surprised recipient of the visitation from a denizen of Hell, was the Duke of Benevento, near Naples, until his death in 787. We also know, from the context of the account in the *Chronicon Salernitanum*, that it was set in the time of Charlemagne (742–814) when a Pope Stephen was on the throne of St Peter. There is actually a choice of three, but Stephen II (752) and Stephen III (752–7) are probably a little too early. On the other hand, the reign of Stephen IV (768–72) fits the bill perfectly. Unfortunately no patriarch of Constantinople was deposed in mysterious circumstances throughout the whole of the latter half of the eighth century, and the briefest reign during the period, that of the Cypriot, Paul IV, was still more than twice the year and a half given for the female patriarch. It seems highly unlikely that she ever existed, but none the less she may have originated in a historical figure, for one of the accusations made by Pope Leo IX in his letter was well-founded.

From 766 to 780, including the years when Stephen IV was Pope, a certain Nicetas held the patriarchate.[11] He was ordained with the approval of the Emperor, even though he was a eunuch and therefore perhaps ineligible for the office, under the first canon of the Council of Nicaea in 325. The case is not entirely clear-cut, however, for the law only barred self-mutilators from the priesthood, and not eunuchs in general as Leo IX claimed. Whether Nicetas' castration was self-inflicted or not, and at what age it took place, is not known.

He was, at any rate, probably unable to grow a beard, and in the Eastern Church where the clergy were forbidden to shave, this would have marked him out as something of an oddity. In consequence he may well have been mocked from time to time as a 'woman'. The belief might also have begun that if a eunuch could become patriarch then so could a member of the female sex. From this it is easy to understand how the story in Erchempert's *Historia Langobardorum* and the *Chronicon Salernitanum* arose.

As we have seen, the fable of the woman patriarch was current by about 890 at the latest. Thus it pre-dates Pope Joan by nearly 400 years. Could it have been transferred from one Church Head to another in the thirteenth century? Despite the fact that it is rather different in the telling, there are some important similarities which would tend to support the possibility. Most noteworthy is the resemblance between the demonic betrayer of the patriarch and the evil spirit in two of the earliest versions of Pope Joan's story, in the *Chronica Minor* and the *Flores Temporum*. Although the devil in these works appears in a different context, its role is otherwise almost identical to that of Arichis' vision.

But why should a tale about a female patriarch, which had been told since the ninth century, suddenly be adapted for the vilification of the Roman pontiff in the thirteenth? The rumours about a woman pope may have spread by word of mouth for a few years before they were written down by Jean de Mailly, so we cannot assume automatically that they began with him. It does seem certain, however, that they originated in eastern France (where Jean de Mailly lived, and Stephen of Bourbon is known to have visited in his official capacity) or Germany, and not in Rome. At this time the papacy had numerous enemies, any of whom could have seen the opportunities offered by the Greek fable and made full use of them, but when the earliest known history of the Pope Joan legend is studied, little doubt remains that the culprits responsible were Franciscan and Dominican friars.

St Francis of Assisi had founded his Order at the start of the century, obtaining papal approval from Innocent III in 1209, just before the Fourth Lateran Council's ban on the formation of new religious orders in 1215. Originally, the Franciscans followed a very strict Rule of poverty, but it was inevitable that as the Order became more of an established institution within the Church, the restrictions on the behaviour and possessions of the friars should be eased with the passage of time. A split occurred between those Franciscans who adapted themselves to conform to a more normal type of organization, and those who still wished for the strict observance of their founder's Rule. The popes, on the whole, favoured the former group, and the friars who remained true to their origins were treated with increasing harshness. This was the more so because many of them were attracted to the dangerous teachings of Joachim of Fiore. Joachim (1145–1202) had taught that the world would go through three cycles, those of the Father, the Son and the Holy Spirit. In the 1250s a book called the *Eternal Gospel* began to circulate. It contained the works of Joachim, together with a prophetic introduction claiming that the Era of the Holy Spirit would be inaugurated in the year 1260, involving a complete collapse of the current ecclesiastical hierarchy. When this did not happen on time, a brisk revision of the dates ensured that Joachim's supporters stayed faithful to the cause, but so blatant a threat to the papacy could not be allowed to continue indefinitely. It was eventually dealt with by John XXII (1316–34), who was promptly branded as the Antichrist for his pains.

The undercurrent of discontent among these groups within the Franciscan brotherhood affected its relationship with the Church in Rome throughout the whole of the latter half of the thirteenth century. The other main order of friars, the Dominicans, founded by the Spaniard Dominic de Guzman at about the same date as the Franciscans, also had their reasons for complaint against the papacy from time to time. In 1254, for instance, Innocent IV upheld the restrictions on their scholastic activities which the University of Paris had imposed when it realized that they were claiming too many privileges and gaining too much power within the system. He also issued the Bull *Etsi animarum*, which deprived them of other freedoms. Soon afterwards Innocent died, and it was widely reported that his death was the direct result of the prayers of the Dominicans, who profited considerably from the accession of his more sympathetic successor.

It must be significant that the first chroniclers of Pope Joan were all friars. Jean de Mailly and Stephen of Bourbon were French Dominicans, while the *Flores Temporum* and the *Chronica Minor* both came from Franciscan friaries in Germany. The tale of the woman pontiff was most probably devised and then perpetuated by individuals within the mendicant orders, as an amusing way of getting their own back for what they saw as their continued unreasonable treatment at the hands of particular popes. As a serious attempt to undermine the authority of the papacy it was doomed to failure, but taken in the spirit in which it was intended—as a scurrilous joke—its durability has been everything its authors could have hoped for.

The bare framework of the initial idea was quickly fleshed out by imaginative embroidery, with background details of a kind familiar from other tales of the Middle Ages. The medieval mind was fascinated by the thought of a woman passing herself off successfully as a man, and thereby enhancing her status in the eyes of God. Any story which included such an imposture was guaranteed instant popularity, and the theme regularly turned up in accounts of the lives of female saints.[12] St Eugenia, for example, was probably a third century Roman martyr, but virtually nothing authentic is known about her. The later legend says that she fled from her Alexandrian household in the guise of a man, accompanied by two servants, SS Protus and Hyacinth, and entered a nearby monastery. There she eventually rose to the office of abbot, but was forced to reveal her sex when a woman whom she had cured of sickness became angry at having her advances refused, and accused the saint of misconduct. Unable to remain in the monastery, Eugenia, together with her newly converted mother and family, travelled to Rome where she was finally beheaded for her faith.

The stories of St Marina, St Theodora, St Margaret Reparata, St Euphrosyne, St Apollinaria (also known as St Hilaria) and St Anastasia Patricia all closely resemble that of Eugenia, but we have no evidence whatever that any of them existed outside the fertile imaginations of the monks who invented them. Marina is said to have lived in a monastery in Bithynia from a very early age. Her father, who was a monk, had taken her there clothed as a boy, and when he died she stayed on, with her sex quite unknown to all, until an innkeeper's daughter claimed that Marina had fathered her child. Unlike Eugenia, she did not immediately prove her innocence by the obvious means, and her feminine sex was discovered only after her decease.

The same predicament faced St Theodora, the wife of Gregory, Prefect of Alexandria. Having taken a lover, she fled in contrition to a monastery, where she lived among the monks for many years in male disguise, till at last a young girl, whom she had rebuffed, spitefully named her as the father of her baby. Choosing not to confess her womanhood, Theodora was expelled and, like Marina, actually adopted the child, bringing it up for some years before returning to the monastery where she was vindicated upon her death. Later her adopted son became the abbot there.

St Anastasia Patricia dressed as a man and willingly withstood the rigours of life as a hermit monk in preference to the amorous attentions of the Emperor Justinian, while St Euphrosyne and St Margaret Reparata had the same motives for their drastic actions although their suitors were rather humbler. This detail aside, St Margaret's history is very similar to that of Eugenia and the others. Accused of immoral conduct, this time with a nun of the convent where she had become 'prior', the truth about her only came to light on her death-bed.

The purity of St Anastasia and St Euphrosyne, on the other hand, was never questioned. It is claimed that for thirty-eight years Euphrosyne lived a blameless life in a monastery near Alexandria, during which time she even heard her own father's confession regularly without being recognized. Anastasia took no such risks, hiding for twenty-eight years in an anchorite's cave and seeing no one.

Euphrosyne, Anastasia and Margaret belong with that large group of female saints who took vows of virginity and suffered martyrdom rather than submit to an undesired marriage with a pagan, as in the popular legend of St Margaret of Antioch who preferred decapitation to matrimony. The most startling of these martyrs to chastity was undoubtedly the imaginary Portuguese princess, St

Uncumber (or Wilgefortis), who, on being faced with a future husband selected by her father, prayed to God for help and was rewarded with a profuse growth of beard. Not unnaturally her father was somewhat put out by this unusual occurrence and had her crucified. The fates of the female monks, who renounced their sex rather less spectacularly, were mild by comparison.

Most of these stories probably derived, at least in part, from the early legend of St Pelagia the Penitent. The connection in the cases of St Margaret and St Marina is certain, for Margaret was called 'Pelagius' by her brothers in Christ, and 'Marina' is no more than the Latin rendering of the Greek 'Pelagia' (of the sea). According to the narrative of 'James the Deacon', Pelagia was a beautiful dancing girl in Antioch, who repented her dissolute life after hearing the preaching of Nonnus, the historical Bishop of Edessa in the middle of the fifth century. She clothed herself in male attire and travelled to the Mount of Olives, where she lived in a cell for the rest of her days, becoming known locally as 'Pelagius, monk and eunuch'. Her secret was only discovered by those who came to bury her body. In amazement they all cried, 'Glory to Thee, Lord Christ, who hast many treasures hidden on the earth, and not men only, but women also.' [13]

Myths of Christian women adopting masculine disguise are almost as old as Christianity itself. Earlier even than St Pelagia was St Thecla, perhaps the most famous of them all. She was reputedly a companion of St Paul, but she is not mentioned in either the Acts of the Apostles or any of St Paul's letters. It is the apocryphal second century *Acts of Paul* which tells how she fled from her betrothed in Iconium in order to follow the apostle, and at one stage, after many adventures, temporarily dressed herself as a boy, sewing 'her mantle into a cloak after the fashion of a man'.

Of all these women only St Eugenia may reasonably be supposed to have existed, and even in her case few details of her legend have any historical accuracy. St Hildegund, however, is rather different. [14] Her existence seems well established, for immediately after she died in 1188 an account of her life was written by a Cistercian Abbot named Engelhard. His source was a monk of Schönau Abbey, near Heidelberg, where the dying Hildegund had confessed her story, omitting only to disclose her sex which was revealed later, and her real name which came to light after posthumous enquiries in the place of her birth. Calling herself 'Joseph', she had entered the monastery as a novice many months previously, having led a remarkably eventful life from early adolescence.

Apparently she was the daughter of a noble couple from Neuss, on the Rhine near Cologne, and always a weakly child. As a thanksgiving for her birth, and perhaps for that of a twin sister, Agnes, her parents vowed to make a pilgrimage to the Holy Land, but the mother died before she could leave, and Hildegund had to take her place. Realizing the dangers of taking a young girl on such a trip, her father sensibly dressed her in the clothing of a boy. They reached Jerusalem safely, but on their way back the father died, and Hildegund, by then known as 'Joseph', was left to cope as best she could. After a number of mishaps she did manage to get back to Germany, but her adventures were far from over. In the employ of an envoy of Archbishop Philip of Cologne, Hildegund was commissioned to carry letters to the Pope, but on the road she was mistaken for a thief and condemned to death, submitted to trial by ordeal, freed and finally hanged by relatives of the real thief. She survived her three days on the gibbet through the intervention of an angel who held her up by the waist and also, presumably by way of passing the time, correctly forecast the date of her death three (or two) years hence. It was some short while after her rescue that she entered the monastery at Schönau, perhaps having become so used to being treated as a man by then that she found it inconceivable to change.

The more miraculous episodes of this account are obviously to be taken with a pinch of salt. Hildegund herself may have invented them, but it is equally likely that the community at Schönau made them up. As Herbert Thurston has pointed out, it was in the monks' best interests to exaggerate such matters in order to show that they had been fooled by a saint rather than an ordinary woman—an ordinary woman, moreover, who had broken the Old Testament law which forbade transvestism as an 'abomination' (Deuteronomy 22:5).

We are on safer ground with her life after she became a novice. There are several early sources which corroborate Engelhard's version of the affair, without actually copying it (see the *Appendix* for full details). Undoubtedly the most influential of these was Caesar of Heisterbach's *Dialogus Miraculorum*. Compiled between 1220 and 1235, this popular collection of gossip and more-or-less moral tales contains a lengthy section on Hildegund, which the author claims to have based on the recollections of one Brother Hermannus, a young fellow-novice of the saint's at Schönau.

The fact that 'Joseph' was female remained unknown until her death, but Caesar reports a certain initial puzzlement on the part of the monastery's abbot: 'When he heard the gentle feminine voice in which she spoke, (he) said to her, "Brother Joseph, has your voice not yet broken?" and she answered: "Sir, I do not think it will ever break"'. She seems to have been ailing for most of the time, but 'she slept among men, with men she ate and drank, with men she bared her back to the scourge' without being detected. However, if Caesar is to be believed, her presence did trouble a few of the monks, one of whom is described as saying, 'This brother of ours is either a woman or a devil, because I have never been able to look at him without temptation.'

Hildegund's illness may have helped protect her from discovery for, in the situation in which she found herself, the hardest thing to disguise would not have been her feminine form, but her periods. If she was sick and ill-nourished when she arrived at the monastery, she may have ceased menstruating altogether, and never returned to her natural rhythm in her final months. It is even possible to theorize further that, in an unconscious effort to avoid maturing into a woman, she had become a victim of anorexia nervosa and never had any periods at all. Perhaps, like St Hilaria, one of the legendary female monks, she was 'shrunken with ascetic practices nor was she subject to the curse of women; since God Almighty ordained for her the thing appointed.'[15]

She must, at any rate, have been very confused and disturbed when she came to Schönau. Having been made to act as a boy at such a formative stage in her childhood, the effect on her would have been profound, especially since she did not originally assume the role from choice. The stress of years of concealment may well have contributed to her early death, whether from anorexia nervosa or some other psychologically based disease. '

There is admittedly no exact parallel to the story of Pope Joan in St Hildegund's history, nor in the fables of the other women we have discussed. The female pope is always portrayed as a far stronger character who is not forced to adopt men's clothing by circumstance, but deliberately chooses to do so in order to gain power and knowledge. Most of the others are obvious victims, usually of male oppression in some shape or form. Nowhere is this more evident than in the very late (and probably historical) case of the Blessed Hugolina, who seems to have lived for forty-seven years as Hugo the hermit, in a cell near Vercelli, in the second half of the thirteenth century. She was only fourteen years old when forced to flee from her family home after her father attempted to commit incest with her.[16]

Pope Joan did not become a victim until the very end of her life. Nevertheless, such tales must undoubtedly have helped in the development of her legend. In particular, the revelations about Hildegund, occurring as they did at the end of the twelfth century and being popularized almost immediately by Caesar of Heisterbach, will have ensured that the idea of a woman passing as a male cleric was less than novel. Small wonder then that Pope Joan, a product of the Rhineland just like Hildegund, was readily accepted when she made her first appearance a few decades later.

5

SCEPTICISM AND POLEMIC

THE popular acceptance of Pope Joan was increasingly enthusiastic, universal and uncritical, but as the Middle Ages drew to a close and the rationalistic humanism of the Renaissance gathered strength, dissenting voices began to be heard. Even in the middle of the fifteenth century there were a few, of whom the most distinguished was Aeneas Sylvius Piccolomini, the future Pope Pius II (1458–64). Although he is famous today for his one great mistake, the attempt to raise the last Crusade, he was a knowledgeable and well-read man who made few such errors of judgement. In 1451, while Bishop of Siena, he wrote to Joannes Carvajalius and referred briefly to the story of the woman pontiff, adding 'nor is it certain history.'[1] Even so, Piccolomini's doubts about Pope Joan were not strong enough to compel him to remove her bust from the cathedral of which he was bishop for seven years.

Similarly in two minds was Bartolomeo Platina, the Prefect of the Vatican library, who expressed his feelings about the tale in 1479. After giving the details which we have quoted elsewhere, he continued:

These things that I have mentioned are popularly told, though by obscure and untrustworthy authors, and therefore I have related them briefly and plainly, so that I should not be thought obstinate and pertinaceous in omitting that which almost everyone asserts to be true.[2]

By the sixteenth century the myth was losing ground fast. The alteration of the bust of 'John VIII, A Woman from England' in Siena Cathedral to one of Pope Zachary, on the order of Clement VIII, is a good instance of this change of heart by the Catholic establishment and literati (if not by the ordinary people). What Aeneas Sylvius Piccolomini could not do in the 1450s, Pope Clement felt perfectly at liberty to authorize 150 years later.

However, by this time the Protestant Reformation was in full swing, and it was not long before its polemicists, ever keen to blacken the papacy and the Roman Catholic Church, realized that the female pope offered an opportunity too good to be missed.

John Jewel, the Bishop of Salisbury (1560–71) under Elizabeth I, was among the first to see the possibilities of this propaganda weapon. In 1567 he wrote his *Defence of the Apology of the Church of England*, as part of a continuing exchange of arguments in print between himself and the Catholic Dr Thomas Harding, a former treasurer and canon-residentiary at Salisbury, who had left the country shortly after Queen Elizabeth's accession. Jewel defended the existence of the woman pope, which Harding had ridiculed previously in his *Confutation* (1565), and simultaneously attacked the papacy, in a diatribe filled with the beautiful rounded prose of the period:

And why might not pope Joan, being a woman, have as good right and interest unto the see of Rome, as afterward had pope John XIII, who, being pope, had wicked company with two of his own sisters; or others, whom for their horrible vices and wickedness Platina called *monstra et portenta*, 'monsters against kind, and ill-shapen creatures'? Luitprandus saith, as it is before reported: *Lateranense palatium . . . nunc (est) prostibulum meretricum*, 'The pope's palace of Lateran in Rome is now become a stew of whores' . . . Yet neither would so many chronicles have recorded, nor would the whole world so universally have believed these things of the pope more than of any other bishop, had there not been wonderful corruption of manners, and dissolution of life, and open horror, and filthiness in that only see above all others.[3]

Thus was Joan damned along with practisers of incest, libertines and other sinners, which seems rather unjust, but it was nothing new for her. Earlier Catholic writers such as Cardinal Torrecremata had often taken the same attitude, counting her as worse and less defensible than a heretic.

It was Harding who had the better of the argument on the reality or otherwise of the female pontiff, but as these extracts show, that was not the point. Jewel was not seriously interested in the historical facts of the matter except to the extent to which they would serve his polemical purpose. This subordination of fact to argument was general among the polemicists on both sides and, as a result, every statement made either for or against Pope Joan in the sixteenth and seventeenth centuries has to be examined very carefully before it can be taken at face value. The dismissal of her story by Cardinal Baronius, shortly after 1600, as a tissue of 'fables without proofs, in every respect lying, mad, absurd, vain, frivolous, loose, contradictory . . .'[4] would, for instance, carry more weight if he had not credited a number of equally unlikely but less embarrassing tales, such as those of the Seven Sleepers of Ephesus and St Ursula's 11,000 Virgins.

Not all Catholics were entirely happy to see Pope Joan removed from the catalogue of the popes after 300 years of acceptance. A few countered the Protestants by maintaining that, while she was real enough, she may not have been truly female. Perhaps, they said, she was a hermaphrodite or even a man whom God had miraculously tranformed into a woman, just as Tiresias, the blind seer of Greek legend, was successively given the body of a man, a woman and then a man again. Why the Almighty should have played such a mean trick on a reigning pontiff they explained by pointing out that God moves in mysterious ways. Their chief motive was, of course, to give some kind of dubious validity to Joan's decisions and acts while Pope; a validity which they would not have had if taken by a mere woman. Naturally enough, Dr Jewel derided the notion, standing out for a completely female Joan as being more awkward for his opponents:

One of your Louvanians would seem handsomely to excuse and shift the matter by possibility of nature. For thus he saith in effect: What if the pope were *hermaphroditus*, an *herkinalson*, that is to say, a man and a woman both in one? Or, if this help will not serve, he seemeth further to say: What if the pope being first a man, were afterward changed into a woman? And thus, for want of better divinity, he forceth Ovid's *Metamorphosis* to serve the turn. If ye would have taken this man's advice, out of doubt with such a pretty 'what if' ye might soon have put us out of countenance. His words be these: 'I will here say nothing of such persons as be called *hermaphroditi*, and are both man and woman all in one; whereof in old writers we find much mention. But, not to go further than to the remembrance of our own time, I know it is written that a certain woman named Aemylia, married unto one Antonius Spensa, a citizen of Ebulum, twelve years after she had been married was turned into a man. I have likewise read of another woman that, when she had been brought a-bed, afterward became a man.' These notable stories he allegeth to answer the matter of pope Joan. Thus he thinketh it a great deal the safer way to make the pope an *herkinalson*, or by miracle to turn him from a man into a woman, than simply and plainly to confess that ever dame Joan was pope in Rome.[5]

The 'Louvanian' referred to by Jewel was Alan Cope, an English Catholic who fled, like Harding and many others of his kind, to the Anti-Reformation stronghold at the University of Louvain in Belgium when Queen Mary died in 1558. The idea that the female pontiff was an androgyne or hermaphrodite seems originally to have come from a book entitled *Dialogi Sex Contra Summi Pontificatos*, which was published at Antwerp in 1566.[6] Although Cope's name was attached to it, he was merely protecting the identity of the true author, his friend Dr Nicholas Harpsfield, who was imprisoned in the Tower of London. Harpsfield had been a Judge of the Court of Arches and prebendary of Canterbury Cathedral, but when Elizabeth I came to the throne he refused to acknowledge the ecclesiastical supremacy of the monarch and was incarcerated for the rest of his days.

Predictably, Harpsfield's quaint hermaphrodite theory became a popular matter for discussion among writers on both sides. The Protestant tract *The Anatomie of Pope Ioane*, published in 1624 with its authorship hidden behind the initials 'I.M.', begins mildly enough by identifying the popes with the Antichrist and the Abomination of Desolation, but after only a few pages it raises the favourite topic:

Certes, this is strange for a man to be turned into a woman: but all things considered, it is nothing strange at all. For the Pope hath all lawes and knowledge within his breast, and whatsoever he be, he is holy, and immaculate, and can worke no small wonders. May not he change himselfe into sundrie shapes, as well as Iupeter, Mercurie, Apollo and other of the Gods? May he not be changed into a woman as well as Tiresias was: or as well as Caietana and Aemilia into men? Yes doubtlesse, for he is farre above them, and can do so much more than ever they could. Therefore Maister Copes surmise, that the Pope may be changed into a woman, is verie Catholicke and substantiall, and fit for such a pregnant and illuminate doctor. But fie for shame, what a sottish excuse is this? What a vaine illusion and Maygame? Is there no better shift nor surer refuge than this? Is there no thicker cloud to spread over the matter with more likelihood? Then who seeth not the bondage of Egypt: who sees not the spirituall Babylon, and the madnesse of them that commit spirituall fornication with her? Better it had bene, and the safer way by a great deale, amplie and plainly to have confessed it, then by a myracle to turne the Pope from a man into a woman, and that which is worst of all, obstinately to defend it. For now everie one doth see, that you had leifer be filthie still, then leave off your filthienesse, and had rather (because you love your vices) excuse them, then forsake them: and as many as in spirit and truth do love the Lord, do mourne for griefe, to see men carried so headlong with such godlesse and retchlesse imaginations. [7]

Such strong language reflects the sheer spitefulness underlying much of the vehemence of Protestant writers in their fervent championing of the existence of the female pontiff. But some Catholics did, undoubtedly, play right into their enemies' hands by adopting the absurd hermaphrodite hypothesis. *The History of Pope Joan and the Whores of Rome*, printed in London in 1687, during the reign of James II when the Catholic cause was enjoying royal support, sensibly stays on safer ground with its refutation of the Protestant point of view. The author, however, is unable to resist lapsing into the occasional polemical passage:

Can any ingenious Person ever believe that such a wise Nation, as the Romans are, and always have been, could be so greatly impos'd upon; or that they should be so Sottish or Stupid, as not one of them to know a Woman from a Man; neither by her Voice, Countenance, nor Costume? And is it not very unlikely, that she should be got with Child now in her declining Age, at which time the Popes are ordinarily Chose? And that she should be ignorant of her being so near her Time, as to venture to go in procession so far on Foot? All very probable, or rather ridiculous Romances. [8]

Unfortunately for the anonymous writer, all of the ideas at which he scoffs so earnestly are perfectly feasible. There are examples from many different eras and places of women who passed themselves off very effectively as men in order to become soldiers, doctors and in at least one case, of course, a monk. There are also numerous incidents of women giving birth unexpectedly; something which seems to be particularly common among the middle-aged, who attribute the cessation of their periods to the menopause (and their weight-gain to over-indulgence). Not that Pope Joan need necessarily have been middle-aged or elderly when she rose to the papacy. John XI was in his teens or early twenties when his mother, Marozia, obtained the throne of St Peter for him in 931, and John XII was a mere eighteen years old on his ascendency in 955. Yet it would be unfair to judge *Pope Joan and the Whores of Rome* in its entirety from this one misguided section alone, for much of it is well-argued and quite sensible, but it does illustrate the tendency of the polemicists to overstate their case, even when they happened to have right on their side.

Soon after the book appeared, James II was forced to abdicate and flee to France. In the far more Protestant climate of 1689, under William III and Mary, the inevitable counterblast was published, signed by one 'R.W.' Couched in rather more restrained language than its predecessors, this *Pope Joan* itemizes no less than thirty-eight 'witnesses' prior to the time of Martin Luther in the sixteenth century, together with some of a later date, to support its argument for Pope Joan's existence. The booklet is naturally most suspect when dealing with the earliest 'witnesses', the first of whom 'R.W.' claims to have been Liudprand of Cremona, writing in about 937. Would that this were so, but regrettably Liudprand knew nothing whatever about a female pontiff. It would be charitable to assume that 'R.W.' was simply confused by Liudprand's accounts of those other powerful women of Rome; the Theophylacts, Marozia and Theodora.

'R.W.', in common with all the other Protestant polemicists, could find no reference to Pope Joan interpolated into the works of any of her supposed contemporaries. Even the insertions in a couple of late editions of Anastasius' *Liber Pontificalis* are never mentioned.

Another polemical tract from the Protestant side was *Pope Joane. A Dialogue Between a Protestant and A Papist*, a highly popular work first issued in 1610 with the author's name, Alexander Cooke, for once given in full. A slightly different version, *A Present for a Papist* by 'A Lover of Truth', was fairly constantly in print from 1675 to 1785. The edition of 1675 has a particularly delightful frontispiece showing a jolly looking Pope Joan giving birth to a chubby, surprised baby, who is peeking out from under her robes. There is a rather cruder mirror-image of this picture in the 1785 revision (opposite). The accompanying rhyme says it all:

> A Woman Pope (as History doth tell)
> In High Procession once in Labour fell,
> And was Deliver'd of a Bastard Son;
> Whence Rome some call The Whore of Babylon.[9]

The Protestant's side of the 'dialogue', as given by Alexander Cooke, is bolstered with all the familiar interpolations in the old chronicles. The poor papist, meanwhile, is given little in the way of solid evidence to support his viewpoint, and his weak theories connecting various Theophylact popes with Joan are easily disposed of by his opponent, who naturally gets the better of the argument. This sort of heavily weighted 'dialogue' was a favourite technique with the pamphlet writers of the sixteenth and seventeenth centuries, and it was by no means limited to the subject of the female pope. M.R. James, in *Abbeys*, quotes

7. Pope Joan in childbirth. From *A Present for a Papist* (1785 edition).

a good example in the form of an Elizabethan ballad which revolves around a disputation between 'Plain Truth' and 'Blind Ignorance' on the subject of monasteries. 'Truth', taking the Protestant part, inevitably succeeds in converting 'Ignorance' to his opinion.[10]

Although we have confined ourselves to examining only the British tracts of this period, it should not be thought that the appearance of Pope Joan in such polemical literature was in any way a phenomenon unique to these islands. As befits the birthplace of the Protestant Reformation, it was Germany which produced the greatest quantity of propaganda in favour of the female pope, including a highly successful, vitriolic tract by 'H.S.' (perhaps Hermann Witekind, a Rector of Heidelberg University) in 1588, which was later translated into English as *Historia De Donne Famose or The Romaine Iubile which happened in the yeare 855* (1599). Almost all the countries of Europe became involved in the controversy to some degree.

After the end of the seventeenth century, the rise of antiquarian research for its own sake coincided with a more reasoned approach to the study of the woman pontiff, and her consequent fading from the realms of religious argument. Nevertheless, a few anti-Catholic authors, right up to the present century, have chosen to introduce her into their discourses in a strictly traditional manner. From August through to November 1876, for example, the *Spalding Free Press* published an exchange of letters between the Revd John Fairfax Francklin and Mr William Clement, which was reminiscent at times of the debate between John Jewel and Thomas Harding 300 years earlier. Francklin was the vicar of Whaplode in Lincolnshire, while Clement, a recent convert to Catholicism, was a former Master of Whaplode Chapel School. Their mutual enmity, which is quite clear to the reader, frequently made them lose sight of the facts in the emotion of their outbursts, and if Clement, in denying the historical reality of Pope Joan, comes out slightly on top, there is little credit in his victory. The letters were collected together into a pamphlet, printed in 1876 under the charmingly obvious title of *The Vicar of Whaplode and 'Pope Joan'*.

More recent still is *The End of the Papacy. Its times completed in the year 1870. Never to rise again into political power over the nations of the Earth. With an Appendix including the History of The Woman Popess Joan*. Such an archaic heading suggests a seventeenth century tract, but in fact this booklet, by Edward Poulson, was provoked by the Vatican Council's declaration of papal infallibility in July 1870, and dates only from 1901. It is surprising to find such vitriolic polemic in favour of the existence of the (tautologically named) 'Woman Popess' cropping up so recently, especially as the evidence for and against her was quite well established at the time. A quotation from the five-page appendix will give the flavour of the work:

The real motive of the Roman Catholics and the Anglican Ritualists in their attempts to obliterate the plain historical records relating to the Popess Joan, is the palpable flaw she makes in the papal succession. The repeated interruptions and breakages in the alleged papal succession by the many schisms of the Popes, when two or three Popes were reigning at one time, would render it impossible to trace any regular succession, but a Woman Popess in the papal chair equals the profligacy of the women whose "gallants" occupied the papal chair in the tenth century, as recorded by Cardinal Baronius.

I have omitted or passed over some of the revolting details and practices relative to the elevation of this Woman to the pontifical chair; but there can be no doubt that the Woman Popess consecrated and ordained many Cardinals, who also in their turn consecrated many Bishops, so that the alleged succession has become seriously complicated. [11]

Clearly Poulson's main purpose was to dispute the Apostolic Succession, and by extension the authority and validity of the entire Catholic Church. He was aware that a real Joan would threaten the succession only if she had herself consecrated bishops, and therefore he took it for granted that this must have occurred, even though the surmise is not directly supported by any of the medieval chronicles which mention her. Had a female pope ruled in Rome, that fact alone would not have endangered the—admittedly shaky—Apostolic line any more than the existence of other pontiffs who, for one reason or another, were not worthy of their position. According to William of Ockham, by the early fourteenth century there had already been twenty-six of these men, excluding Joan, who had 'assumed the papacy but afterwards committed wicked and embarrassing crimes such as idolatry, usurpation, simony, nepotism, heretical perversity, blasphemy, fornication and many other enormities'.[12] William, as a Franciscan, was not one of the pope's greatest supporters so we must allow for a certain exaggeration here, but even so, if the worst of these twenty-six were not removed from the records, then there would seem to be no reason why Pope Joan alone should have been obliterated from history in order to protect the Apostolic Succession.

Nowhere does Poulson enlarge upon his reference to the 'plain historical records' of the female pontiff, and in this he is a typical polemicist. Throughout the years in which religious polemic prospered, it can safely be said that it added little or nothing to the serious investigation of our subject.

6

MODERN TIMES

MOST sixteenth and seventeenth century Protestants considered that their cause was best served by stoutly defending the reality of Pope Joan. Nevertheless it was a French Protestant minister who wrote the first full-length book devoted to the opposite viewpoint, arguing the case for dismissing the story as pure invention. David Blondel's *Familier Eclaircissement de la Question, Si une femme a esté assise au Siege Papal de Rome entre Leon IV & Benoist III* was published in 1647, and either studiously ignored or greeted with horror by the polemicists. It certainly did nothing to check their outpourings.

His fellow-countryman Pierre Bayle, some fifty or so years later, described the widespead feeling that Blondel had been misguided in his efforts to reveal the fictional nature of the woman pontiff. Many people protested that:

The Protestant Interest requires it should be true, why must a Minister discover the falsity of it? Would it not have been better to leave the Papists the trouble of wiping their own filth away? Did they, who do not cease to reproach the Memory of the Reformers, deserve that any one should do them that good office. [1]

Blondel's work was a particularly important one in that, unlike the Catholic authors, he could not easily be accused of unreasonable bias, although this did not prevent some of his contemporaries from seeking to find a devious motive for his actions. It would seem that he simply wished to establish the truth of the matter, but not everyone was willing to believe or understand this. Blondel was a man ahead of his time, but over the next 150 years, many others followed his lead and wrote studies which were, by and large, fairly honest and intelligent, even though they all suffered from the lack of some important sources which were not then available.

The title of Blondel's book shows that he confined himself to the question of whether a female pope reigned between Leo IV and Benedict III, without considering the possibility that she might have ruled at some other date. The historians of the seventeenth and eighteenth centuries did not have access to the treatises of Jean de Mailly and Stephen of Bourbon, which place the woman pontiff around 1100, so they naturally assumed that the old chroniclers agreed unanimously in locating her reign in the ninth century. The inevitable result of this general ignorance, was that they tended to spend a disproportionate amount of their time in showing that there was no suitable gap between Leo IV and Benedict III into which the female pope might be fitted.

The Dominican Michel Le Quien (1661–1733), for instance, devoted eighty columns of his *Oriens Christianus*, published posthumously in 1745, to Pope Joan. At least a quarter of them are concerned solely with listing and describing large numbers of letters and other ninth century documents which do not mention her. Useful as this is, it only goes part of the way to proving that she did not exist, and it is far from the complete answer which Le Quien thought it was. Within their limits, however, Blondel and those who followed him can only occasionally be seriously faulted on their interpretation of the facts.

Not every writer at this time held rigidly dogmatic views. John Laurence Mosheim in his *Ecclesiastical History*, which was compiled during the last half of the eighteenth century, tried hard to be fair to all sides, and suggested that some unusual event must have happened in the 850s to give rise to the story: 'But what it was . . . is yet to be discovered, and is likely to remain uncertain'. Mosheim would perhaps have gone along with the opinion expressed by the great philosopher G.W. Leibnitz, several decades previously, in a tongue-in-cheek attack on what he saw as the wrong-headedness of the Catholic viewpoint. His idea was that an important ninth century bishop called John Anglicus may indeed have given birth to a child in full view of everyone on the streets of Rome, but that this bishop was not and never had been the pope.[2] Of course, there is no evidence whatever for this, as Leibnitz himself well knew. His theory has been taken literally by far too many subsequent authors, who seem to have missed his note of sarcasm.

The superficially well-balanced position of Mosheim was, in fact, based on the patently false premise that the event in question was 'universally believed and related in the same manner by a multitude of historians, during five centuries immediately succeeding its supposed date . . . nor, before the reformation undertaken by Luther, was it considered by any, either as incredible in itself, or as disgraceful to the church'.[3] That Mosheim managed to avoid the excesses of either side in the controversy is to his credit, but it proves nothing. If he had studied the researches of his ostensibly more extreme contemporaries with greater care, he might have realized how mistaken he was in some of his assumptions.

By 1863, when John J.I. Von Döllinger, Professor of Theology at the University of Munich, wrote his long chapter on the female pontiff in *Die Pabstfabeln des Mittelalters* (*Fables Respecting the Popes of the Middle Ages*), a wider variety of material was available and Döllinger was able to make an acceptably thorough analysis of the subject, marred only by his exceedingly dour and humourless style, and his belief that Jean de Mailly's *Chronica Universalis* was 'lost, or as yet undiscovered'.[4] Since he was aware of the chronicle of Stephen of Bourbon, his argument did not suffer greatly from the omission.

That most peculiar of Victorian High-Church Anglicans, Sabine Baring-Gould, who was Rector of Lew Trenchard in Devon and a prolific writer of fiction and non-fiction alike, devoted a chapter in his *Curious Myths of the Middle Ages* to 'Antichrist and Pope Joan',[5] linking these two legendary figures by means of certain old authorities who, he said, had stated that the female pope's child was the very Antichrist himself. Unfortunately the authorities are not identified, and we have been totally unable to trace them, which is disappointing since the theory is an intriguing and dramatic one. It is not supported by any of the early sources, only one of which hints at the later life of Pope Joan's son, saying that he became the Bishop of Ostia. However, it may have been invented by the Protestant polemicists, whose outpourings were so numerous that we have been quite unable to examine them all. According to Baring-Gould, some of the works to which he referred went on to maintain that the baby Antichrist was immediately spirited away to reappear in the Last Days, which would explain why he has not yet made his presence felt. In view of Baring-Gould's irritating failure to document his sources, little more can be said.

No doubt it was partly the connection with the Antichrist which caused Baring-Gould to see the female pontiff as a personification of the Scarlet Woman of Revelation. His attacks on those, like Mosheim, who were less certain of her unreality, are scathing in the extreme. This was a man who knew absolutely that he was right.

Throughout the nineteenth century, and even disregarding the polemicists, there was still an occasional lone voice crying out in favour of Pope Joan, and a few had sincere reasons for doing so. The Greek author, Emmanuel Rhöides, was so fascinated by the image of the woman pope that he wrote an influential novel about her, which we will discuss in the next chapter. In addition he produced a learned and stylish examination of the subject, coming to the conclusion that she had definitely existed. It seems that Rhöides was blinded to the arguments against Joan, and to the flaws in his own case, by nothing more sinister than his overwhelming affection for her. The book was published in English translation in 1886, and it is amusing to note that the translator found it necessary to censor some of the more earthy passages of the original, which were presumably not thought suitable for the eyes of young Victorian ladies. The section which discusses the pierced seat is severely curtailed with the excuse that 'the details are not fit for publication'.[6]

In the present century, until the late 1960s, the story of the female pope was acknowledged by almost everyone to be completely fictional. Those writers who disagreed with the consensus usually had fairly obvious motives for doing so, as was the case with Clement Wood, an American whose novel of 1931, *The Woman Who Was Pope*, begins with a lengthy introduction. It is largely an exercise in anti-Catholic propaganda, using a variety of secondary sources to 'prove' the reality of Pope Joan. Not content with this, Wood proceeds to disparage the papacy at every opportunity, insisting among other things that Marozia, the Theophylact mother of John XI (931–5), committed incest with practically all the male members of her family, including her grandson, the future Pope John XII (955–63). Actually, when John XII was born in 937, his grandmother was already dead, a minor detail which appears to have escaped Wood's notice.

In complete contrast, the level-headed Jesuit, Herbert Thurston, produced a very valuable little booklet entitled *Pope Joan* for the Catholic Truth Society in 1917, which set the tone for future examinations of the legend. Thurston's assumption that his subject had no historical basis was perhaps inevitable in view of his audience, but the strikingly unbiased nature of his research might come as a surprise to those who have not encountered his work elsewhere. In his time he brought his keen intellect and healthy scepticism to bear on matters as varied as witchcraft, the Turin Shroud and the woman monk, St Hildegund. With Pope Joan he concentrated in particular on British chronicles and books, some of which had previously been completely overlooked, and thus produced a pamphlet containing much original information.

The same, generally accepted, opinion can be found in the entries for the female pope in most modern encyclopedias, and also in a disappointing, error-filled and derivative article in the often thought-provoking part-work, *The Unexplained*. Curiously, the *Encyclopaedia Britannica* and one or two others call her 'John Angelicus' instead of 'John Anglicus', a name-change which neatly side-steps the problem of why the so-called 'John English' should have come from Mainz in Germany. What a shame it never occurred to any of the medieval chroniclers, who went to such efforts to explain the apparent inconsistency by different means. No doubt the angelic John was the result of a printing or transcription error, and not an inspiration on the part of the encyclopedia compiler, but once in print a mistake like this tends to be copied so often that it takes on a reality of its own. We have probably not seen the last of 'John Angelicus'.

As the twentieth century wore on, it began to look as though the questions surrounding the female pontiff had all been answered to everybody's satisfaction. The resolution of G.K. Chesterton's Father Brown story, 'The Doom of the Darnaways', depends on the certainty that a 'cultivated' man would know that 'there was no such person as Pope Joan'. But in the 1960s a new force appeared on the scene, which was to make her story once again the subject of controversy.

One of the many achievements of the feminist movement has been a complete and long overdue re-evaluation of the role of women in history. Influential and important women so often ignored, patronized and insulted by the textbooks have finally started to receive the credit they deserve. This enrichment of our knowledge of the past is a very welcome development, but regrettably, alongside the real figures, a small number of women whose historical standing is, to put it mildly, more than a little doubtful have been taken to the hearts of feminists. Among these is Pope Joan.

A minority—and it is only a minority—of the movement's historians seem to believe that it is perfectly acceptable to distort the facts, in order to counteract and set-off the widespread distortions of the truth, which are undeniably present in the standard patriarchal works. Looked at unemotionally, there can be no justification for this. In the long run it just provides an excuse for people to ignore all feminist research, including much which is balanced and sensible but still equally provocative. The unfortunate result of applying the technique to the female pontiff has been that today a great many women accept her reality as conclusively proven.

Ironically, the first book to take a definite feminist tone in its analysis of the story was written by a man. Henri Perrodo-Le Moyne's *Un Pape Nommé Jeanne* was published in 1972 and appears at first glance to be a fairly straightforward study. The careful reader, however, soon notices that Perrodo-Le Moyne has selected the evidence which agrees with his thesis and ignored or perverted that which does not. In other words, the method of the Protestant polemicists has again reared its ugly head, but this time better disguised and with a different aim. The author's misrepresentations of the facts are often wondrous to behold, as when he maintains that Leo IX's important letter of 1054 to Michael, the Patriarch of Constantinople, mentions the female pope. As we have seen, quite the opposite is true: the letter shows that she had not yet been heard of at that date.

Perrodo-Le Moyne's motives are made perfectly clear by the final section of the book, which is entitled *Femmes, Levez-vous!*' (Women, Arise!), and we are left in no doubt whatsoever by such statements as 'The day when woman frees herself, that day she will no longer be the "spare rib" . . . the papacy and the Church in its entirety will no longer blush concerning John VIII, the Papessa'.

A recurrent and popular theme in this type of work is the supposed conspiracy of silence about Pope Joan, of which the Church is said to have been guilty for many centuries. Some writers limit the plot to the 400 years before 1250, when she made her first appearance in the chronicles, but others extend it further, even down to the present day. Thus Perrodo-Le Moyne relates how he consulted a prelate at the Vatican who told him that 'some very important documents concerning this woman are secretly concealed in chests and under the papal seal'.[7] Again, in Elizabeth Gould Davis' ultra-polemical *The First Sex*,[8] this idea crops up with the claim that in 1601, Pope Clement VIII ordered 'all effigies, busts, statues, shrines and records of her utterly demolished and her name erased from the papal rolls'.

What the conspiracy theorists choose not to recognize, is that it would have taken a great deal more than a couple of hours of labour in the Vatican Library to delete all references to Joan from the pre-thirteenth century sources. It would have required the connivance of thousands of people throughout the known world, including both the Western and Eastern Churches. A conspiracy on this scale appeals to the paranoid in us all, but it hardly seems likely. Nevertheless, if by some massive suspension of disbelief we assume for the sake of argument that it might have been possible, then we can begin to wonder how the erasures were carried out. Were the appropriate sections of the various letters, documents and chronicles simply crossed out or cut away? We could easily detect such censorship today, but needless to say there is no sign of it. On the contrary, when ancient chronicles and papal catalogues have been tampered with in connection with the female pontiff, it has always been in order to insert her where she did not originally appear.

Perhaps, instead, everything mentioning her was collected up and locked away permanently in a forgotten corner of the Vatican, just as Perrodo-Le Moyne would have us believe on the evidence of his anonymous prelate. There is no easy way to prove or disprove such an allegation. The famous 'Secret Archives' of the Vatican are largely secret only in that they were until recently very badly indexed, or worse, not indexed at all, thus making access to particular documents almost impossible. The more modern indexing techniques increasingly being used in the archives today, should surely have brought to light some pre-thirteenth century material concerning Pope Joan by now, were it there to be found. Believers in sinister plots notwithstanding, it would be difficult to suppress news of such a discovery.

The hypothesis that all the records containing information about the woman pope were either locked away or destroyed wholesale raises a further problem. Quite a large number of sources for the period from the ninth to the twelfth century are still extant, but none of them gives any hint of her existence, except in the few cases where it has been added at a later date. So remarkable an event as the birth of a papal child in procession to the Lateran, should have been commented on by all who had occasion to refer to the papacy; and in a fairly short time the tale would have spread all over Europe in the regular correspondence of the literate classes. Yet it does not feature in even the most complete holograph manuscripts.

It might be argued that those writers who were sympathetic to the papacy would have refrained from discussing Pope Joan openly, out of a desire to spare the incumbent pontiff any embarrassment. Reasonable as this is, it does not account for her total absence from the letters and discourses of people who were, for one reason or another, ill-disposed towards the Roman church. If Joan had truly existed, neither Patriarch Photius of Constantinople in the ninth century, nor his successor Michael Cerularius some 200 years later, would have passed up such an opportunity for some excellent anti-Roman propaganda.

Clement Wood has a solution of sorts to this difficulty.[9] Conveniently disregarding the female pope's public parturition, he suggests that only one or two cardinals ever found out her secret, their knowledge being handed down by word of mouth until its eventual revelation in the thirteenth century. Up to then 'Pope John' would have been thought of as a wise and pious pontiff; a worthy if unexciting Bishop of Rome who held no interest for those seeking scandal to show the Church in a bad light. But Wood does not follow his explanation through to its logical and obvious conclusion. If almost everybody thought that Joan was a perfectly normal man, there would have been no reason to exclude her from the papal catalogues, at least for the first 400 years after her death, during the time when the truth was known only to a select few. Her contemporaries and near-contemporaries would also, no doubt, have mentioned the virtuous 'Pope John' now and then in their documents.

There were other authors beside the enemies of Rome who might be expected to have made some comment on the story of Pope Joan. Although such men as William of Malmesbury (c.1080–1142) were faithful Catholics, they refused to allow their respect for the papacy to interfere with their enjoyment of a good tale, even when it was derogatory to a particular pope. The much-maligned Sylvester II (999–1003) was probably the worst sufferer at the hands of the gossip-mongering chroniclers, and the results of his supposed compact with the Devil, were described in increasingly colourful detail, starting one hundred or so years after the end of his reign. William of Malmesbury's *Gesta Regum Anglorum*, written between 1118 and 1125, tells the tale at great length and with obvious relish. Sylvester, or Gerbert of Aurillac, was—it says—a monk of Fleury (St Benoît-sur-Loire) who studied magic at Toledo and rose to St Peter's Chair, assisted by demonic forces: 'So did he urge his fortunes with the Devil's patronage, that nothing which he ever planned was left unfinished'.[10] He constructed one of the brazen heads so beloved of medieval spinners of yarns, but eventually met a horrible end through the trickery of his attendant demons.

Of course, the legend has no basis in fact, and must have grown out of the unwillingness of Sylvester's contemporaries to attribute his unusually extensive learning merely to the natural quickness of his mind. In an era when the popes were not noted for their scholarship, Gerbert was a true polymath; a Renaissance man born five centuries too soon.

If such stories about Sylvester could spread unsuppressed, and be told by writers who saw no paradox in attacking individual pontiffs while still supporting the Church as a whole, then the subject of Pope Joan would hardly have posed any ethical problems either. William of Malmesbury, in particular, should have been fascinated by 'John Anglicus' because of her apparent English ancestry. Yet he is silent about her, and so are all his fellow-countrymen until the start of the fourteenth century.

Similarly, Vincent of Beauvais in the *Speculum Majus* relates the adventures of Sylvester II, while entirely omitting any mention of the female pope. His chronicle was written in about 1254; around the same time as Joan's first recorded appearance, in Jean de Mailly's *Chronica Universalis Mettensis*. If Vincent, a Paris Dominican, had known about her he would almost certainly have included her in his history. His ignorance suggests that Jean de Mailly either invented the account himself or adapted it from oral sources strictly localized in the Metz area of eastern France. As late as the 1250s there seems to have been no popular or widespread tradition, even within the mendicant orders.

The final flaw in the 'conspiracy of silence' theory is simply that references to the woman pontiff occur in a great many works compiled from the late thirteenth century onwards, and no attempt has ever been made to conceal or censor these. In order to explain this sudden abundance of material, more than one person has put forward the idea that a secret Papal Bull was issued around this date, informing all members of the Church that they were now free to reveal the hidden truth about Joan. Why it should have been issued at a time when the papacy was certainly no more, and perhaps rather less, secure than it had been for the preceding centuries is not clear. Anyway, the concept of such a Bull is too ridiculous to contemplate, for its currency would have had to be so wide that it could scarcely have been regarded as 'secret', and it would surely have been preserved somewhere, or left detectable traces.

The existence of all the later sources creates particular difficulties when Elizabeth Gould Davis' claim about Clement VIII is considered. If, as she says, he ordered the destruction of every record of Pope Joan in 1601, then why on earth should his order have been applied only to those dating from before the late 1200s? Why were the remainder tolerated? It is true that during Clement's reign (1592–1605) the bust of *Johannes VIII, Foemina de Anglia* in Siena Cathedral was altered to one of Pope Zachary, but to suggest that this was part of a massive campaign to purge the Church of all knowledge of her is sheer foolishness.

The four pages devoted to the female pontiff in Gould Davis' *The First Sex* are crammed with similar fudged facts and dubious evidence. Without a doubt the book is the worst and most blatant example of its kind. Thus, we read that the mythical two-year gap between the pontificates of Leo IV and Benedict III can easily be found by anyone with 'sufficient interest to look up the facts'. It is certain, we are also told, that Joan's contemporary, Anastasius the Librarian, was among the writers who mentioned her; while the pierced seat was introduced into the ritual of papal enthronement in 855 'and *not before*' (Gould Davis' italics). That the first use of the various seats is well attested to have been in 1099, and to have involved no ceremonial sexing of the pope-elect, is a point which seems to have passed the author by. She also tries to make something out of the slight confusion into which the numbering of the various popes named John has fallen over the centuries. If only to clarify the situation, this matter does deserve some attention here, although in reality it is totally unconnected with the female pontiff.

To begin with, Gould Davis is unique in her belief that the acknowledged existence of two popes named John XXIII, separated in time by over 500 years, was the result of Pope Joan's imposture. The first of the two ruled 1410–15, and was responsible for the condemnation and burning of John Hus as a heretic. This happened during the Great Schism within the papacy, in the last years of which there were three popes reigning simultaneously, all claiming legitimacy for their line of succession; one based in Rome, one in Avignon and the third in Pisa. The Schism finally became so scandalous and confusing that it simply had to be resolved, and this end was achieved by the Council of Constance in 1417 when it elected Martin V to the pontificate. The settlement reached led to all the popes of the Avignon and Pisan lines being counted as antipopes, and their names and numbers were therefore available for re-use. John XXIII was one of the Pisan Obediance, so Angelo Giuseppe Roncalli was able to take the same name, when he was chosen to succeed Pius XII in 1958. For identical reasons there have been two popes Benedict XIII, Clement VII and Clement VIII. Indeed, the only antipope from the Schism whose number has not reappeared is Alexander V.

Curiously enough the matter of the second John XXIII has also attracted the interest of Baigent, Leigh and Lincoln, the authors of *The Holy Blood and The Holy Grail* (1982). Their explanation links the mystery with Rosicrucianism, but ignores the fact that there is really no mystery to explain.

A more intriguing and superficially more puzzling problem is the omission of any Pope John XX from the official list. John XIX died in 1032 and John XXI became supreme pontiff in 1276, but between these dates there was no other pope called John. Gould Davis explains this by proposing that, around the time of John XXI, it was decided to remove Pope Joan (alias John VIII) from the catalogue. Consequently all the other popes with the same name had to be moved back one number, leaving a gap which was never filled—at least not until a feeble attempt was made to do something about it in the present century with the selection of the new John XXIII. In support of the theory, she is forced to resort to statements which are entirely without foundation. Assertions like 'the Pope John (872–82) who is *now* numbered eighth was for seven centuries listed as number nine' are too easily disprovable to help her argument.

The true cause of the missing John XX is not to be found with John VIII in the ninth century, for no pope named John up to and including the fourteenth of that title has ever been renumbered. What seems to have happened is that, in the era of John XXI, a belief grew up that an additional pope had ruled briefly between John XIV (983–4) and John XV (985–96), within the one year gap when the See of Rome was actually in the hands of the antipope Boniface VII. Our old friend Martin Polonus, in his *Chronicon* written in the 1270s, lists this non-existent pontiff under 985 and gives him the title of John XV, adding 'of Roman birth, he reigned for four months'.[11] Thus to Martin Polonus the real John XV became John XVI, despite the contemporary evidence to the contrary, and each of the subsequent Johns had his number increased by one, so that John XIX was changed into John XX. Obviously John XXI accepted this prevailing opinion on the authenticity of his mythical predecessor, and took account of him when nominating his own title. Yet it is undoubtedly true that the mysterious John, 'son of Robertus',[12] never sat in St Peter's Chair and was not inserted into the papal lists until long after his supposed reign. In the beginning he was probably no more than a copyist's error, perhaps arising from the fact that in 984 John XIV spent the final *four months* of his short, eight month rule languishing in prison in the Castel Sant'Angelo, placed there by antipope Boniface.[13] The various popes John, from John XV onwards have since had the original numbers which they bore during their lifetime restored to them, and so there is now no John XX. The responsibility for the gap can be placed squarely on the shoulders of John XXI whose only other claim to fame is the manner of his death in 1277. He was crushed when part of the pope's palace at Viterbo fell on him.

Remembering that all the earliest proponents of Pope Joan, and many later ones too, failed to give her a number and insisted that she was never officially counted in the papal catalogues, it is difficult in any case to see quite what Gould Davis was trying to prove with her unnecessary and untenable theory.

Henri Perrodo-Le Moyne's *Un Pape Nommé Jeanne*, does at least show a reasonable background knowledge of the female pope legend, although the author has shamelessly perverted it to his own ends. For Elizabeth Gould Davis' book not even this can be said. *The First Sex* deals with innumerable women in history, and the section on Joan is a small one, but this can be no excuse for the use of only two sources, both modern, in its composition. An old edition of the *Catholic Encyclopedia*, together with Baring-Gould's quaint *Curious Myths of the Middle Ages*, can hardly have provided a thorough grounding from which to work, although they are evidently quite sufficient for Gould Davis' propagandist purpose.

She concludes with a comment inspired by Baring-Gould's suggestion that the female pontiff was a personification of the Great Whore of Babylon. 'Thus is history rewritten by the masculists', she cries; an accusation not entirely unreasonable in the case of Baring-Gould, whose hatred of women is revealed again and again in his other works. In the fantasy short story, 'The Merewigs',[14] for instance, his attack on those 'blue-stockings' who dared to frequent the library at the British Museum is almost pathological in its intensity. However, Gould Davis seems unaware that Baring-Gould cannot, by any stretch of the imagination, be considered an average representative of the establishment, 'masculist' or otherwise.

There is a displeasing tone to some feminist writing about Pope Joan, which is at times almost indistinguishable from the equally unhelpful Protestant polemic of an earlier age. Elizabeth Gould Davis is an extreme example, and not highly thought of even among other historians within the women's movement, but her views are by no means unique. Even in perfectly sensible feminist publications, the female pope often crops up in statements like 'Pope John VIII was a biological woman',[15] which show no appreciation of the arguments against her existence. The feminist movement does not need to resort to such a mythical and (literally) man-made figure to strengthen its case.

7

THE FICTIONAL JOAN

IN 1982, Caryl Churchill's feminist play *Top Girls* was staged in London. Part of it took the form of a dinner party attended by a number of historical and pseudo-historical female characters, each of whom gave an account of herself. One of those characters was Pope Joan. Her appearance in drama is no novelty, however, for it goes back at least as far as the fifteenth century when Dietrich Schernberg, an Imperial notary at Mühlhausen, wrote *Ein Schön Spiel von Frau Jutten*, which was first published in 1565 but probably completed some seventy-five years earlier. Much of this well-known late medieval play takes place outside the usual confines of the tale of the female pope, who is here called 'Jutta', the German contraction of 'Joan' and one of the first uses of the name.

The play begins with a long scene showing the inhabitants of Hell about their daily business. A decision is made to employ Jutta to further the purposes of the infernal powers, and she is persuaded by the demons Spiegelglanz (looking-glass) and Sathanas to sign a pact with the Devil, on the promise of 'great glory'. After studying in male disguise at the University of Paris—a rather more sensible choice than Athens, incidentally, even though the various Church Schools in the city were not actually organized into a University until the end of the twelfth century—she graduates and travels to Rome with her male companion, Clericus. There, a short time afterwards, they are both made cardinals and, on the death of the incumbent pope, Jutta is elected as his successor; but her rule is destined to be a brief one. She is soon unmasked as a woman and killed, her soul sinking to the depths of Hell in acute despair. In a final scene of great dramatic power she is saved by the intercession of the Virgin Mary and reconciled with God.

Schernberg's 'Jutta' is quite unlike the legendary Pope Joan, whose powers are only occasionally attributed to demonic influence. She is, instead, firmly in the tradition of such popular medieval myths as those of Theophilus and Faust. Theophilus of Adana is said to have been a Christian, who signed away his soul to the Devil after being persecuted by his bishop. Eventually seeing the error of his ways, he was saved by the Virgin Mary who interceded on his behalf and recovered the written contract. The Virgin's role here is practically identical to that which she plays in Schernberg's drama. The image of the Mother of Christ as intercessor between her son and erring humanity had particular potency in the late Middle Ages.

There is a possibility that Goethe was familiar with *Frau Jutten* and had it in mind when he wrote some parts of his eighteenth-century version of the Faust legend. The juxtaposition of certain of his scenes echoes Schernberg, and it has been suggested that Goethe's 'Gretchen' was inspired by Jutta,[1] although definite proof of this has not been forthcoming.

The earliest known English play about Pope Joan was not new when it was performed by Lord Strange's Men at the Rose Theatre in London around March 1591/2, and recorded then (as 'poope Jone') in Philip Henslowe's Diary.[2] The Elizabethan custom was, of course, to have an all-male cast, and one wonders how effective a man could have been in the title role. It was not unusual at the time for a female character to adopt male clothing temporarily (Imogen in *Cymbeline* and Julia in *Two Gentlemen of Verona* are notable examples), but to sustain the double deception for an entire performance must have put considerable strain both on the actor and on the audience's ability to suspend its disbelief. The drama of 'poope Jone' has been lost to posterity, but luckily Elkanah Settle's *The Female Prelate*, staged at the Theatre Royal in 1680, has not suffered the same fate. It contains a portrayal of the woman pontiff very different from Schernberg's, and totally unsympathetic; here she deserves no forgiveness from Heaven, nor does she get any. 'John, Lord Cardinal of Rhemes, originally a German Lady, named Joanna Anglica' is depicted as highly immoral and, indeed, positively murderous.

As the play opens she has already poisoned the old Duke of Saxony, ostensibly because of his Protestant leanings. His son, the current Duke, is in Rome and unsuccessfully accuses Cardinal John of committing the murder. Saxony is arrested for his pains, while Joanna becomes the new pope. A good deal of intrigue on both sides follows, during which Joanna disguises herself as Saxony's wife and shares his bed, only to be disturbed by the ghost of the old Duke. The pope then sends her page, Amiran, to poison the young Duke, but instead Amiran reveals the truth of Joanna's sex to him.

Armed with this information, Saxony tries to turn the Roman populace against Pope Joan by proclaiming her secret publicly, but when he attempts to kill her he is prevented and taken away to be burned. Meanwhile Joanna, in the customary fashion, miscarries in procession and dies. The play ends with the cardinals agreeing to institute the ceremony of the pierced seat:

> Thus then the Coronation Porphyry,
> On which Romes installed Bishop, Heavens
> Lieutenant takes his great Commission,
> Shall thro' it have that subtle concave form'd
> Thro' which a reverend Matrons hand . . .[3]

(This is a startling new twist to the story: the sexing of the pope-elect is to be done, not by the junior deacon present, but by a 'reverend matron'!)

Unfortunately a plan to reprint the play in an edition by Montague Summers, which was announced some years ago, never came to fruition. Although not a great work, *The Female Prelate* remains the most interesting of Elkanah Settle's prolific output (*The Conquest of China, by the Tartars* and *Ibrahim the Illustrious Bassa* are among many others), and it does not deserve its present obscurity.

A century after *The Female Prelate*, and across the English Channel in Paris, there seems to have been something of a fashion for vaudeville plays about the woman pontiff. One of these was the charming *La Papesse Jeanne* by C. Fauconpret, printed in 1793. Its introduction, 'Pope Joan to her readers. The story of my journeys', retails the author's efforts to have his work staged; efforts which were apparently doomed to failure even though 'other Popes Joan were appearing in two of the theatres of the capital' at the time.

La Papesse Jeanne is pure farce, related in a kind of doggerel which translates very readily into English. The action commences with a debate among the College of Cardinals as they meet to elect a new pope. Eventually Joan, a busy and ambitious lady whose lovers include Mafféo and Morini, the leaders of the two major factions of the Sacred College, is chosen when agreement cannot be reached on any other candidate. The cardinals soon regret their decision, however, and in the final scene of the play, news is brought to them of Joan's giving birth while in procession:

Attendant   How the people will smirk and shout
           When this story at last is out.
           We approached Saint John's, we were nearly there,
           When a horrid event threw us into despair.
           The procession was halted; feet slid around;
           Thud! the pope fell down to the ground.

           The holy father groaned and shouted,
           The fear in the crowd was quite undoubted;
           Who could help him? Was there none?
           Suddenly the pope . . . gave birth to a son.[4]

The cardinals are told that the indignation of the Roman mob is now directed towards themselves. Fearing for their lives, they flee via the window:

Attendant   Ah! My Lords, there's more to it yet;
           The people are wild, and coming to get
           Revenge; so if you'll take my advice
           You'll all of you leave; I'll be gone in a trice.
           I'm not staying around; you'll be wise to go too.
           Accepting their anger you'll not want to do.

Cardinals   How can we go? What means do we need?

Attendant   It's the window for me—so follow my lead.
          (He jumps through the window).

Cardinals   Quickly! Quickly! Let's take his advice!

Maffèo   I think in future we'd best not fail,
          To avoid a repeat of this dreadful tale,
          To seek clear proofs our pope is male.
          (They all jump out of the window).

It would be impossible to find a greater contrast to these delightfully silly verses than the 1972 film *Pope Joan*, directed by Michael Anderson, which treats the legend with an overwhelming seriousness quite unleavened by humour. The heavy-handed style is leaden and often tedious, despite a believable and intelligent performance by Liv Ullman in the title role. John Briley, the writer of the screenplay, was to win an Oscar eleven years later for his work on Richard Attenborough's *Gandhi*. Perhaps he would prefer to forget his earlier effort. For *Pope Joan* he invented most of the plot himself, ranging widely from the traditional story and incorporating some unpleasant additions including a gratuitous gang-rape of Joan by several monks, and outbreaks of a vicious kind of Wotan-worship. The one original twist of undeniable appeal is to make the father of the pope's child, not the monk who had travelled with her from Germany, but the Holy Roman Emperor (played by Franco Nero) himself.

For some reason the film was called *The Devil's Imposter* in the United States: a more dramatic title admittedly, but hardly an accurate one, for Liv Ullman's Joan gains her power entirely without the intervention of demonic forces. Indeed, *Pope Joan* would have benefited considerably from the introduction of an occasional supernatural interlude to break up its desperate and tenuous facade of authenticity. Originally the intention was to intersperse the historical scenes with modern ones, featuring a young woman suffering from the delusion that she is Pope Joan. The extra material was shot but not used in the final film, and it is difficult to say whether it would have made any improvement in practice. It could hardly have made the film worse, at any rate.

Visual interpretations of the female pope's life go back a long way, but it was not until the late nineteenth century that biographical novelists recognized her potential as a subject. One of the earliest, and certainly the one with the most lasting influence, was the Greek writer Emmanuel Rhöides, who was born in 1835. His novel, *Pope Joan: A Romantic Biography*, first appeared in print (as *Papissa Joanna*) in 1886, and there was a immediate furore, caused as much by the author's biting satire on the Church in general as by his portrayal of the woman pontiff. The book was banned in Greece and Rhöides was excommunicated by the Orthodox Church. The success of the story was thereby assured, and the first French edition sold several hundred thousand copies. It has twice been translated into English, most recently by Lawrence Durrell in 1954. Durrell's stylish version has even found its way quite recently into paperback; firm evidence of the book's durability.

Rhöides was an avowed believer in the existence of the woman pope, but fortunately his novel is much more than mere propaganda. It is an entertaining and skilfully written work, based on the traditional legend and incorporating all the stories told about Joan in the fourteenth and fifteenth centuries, as well as a number of details completely original to Rhöides but now frequently and quite mistakenly assumed to be older. Some incidents previously attached to other people are also included. As a tiny baby in 818, for instance, 'Joanna' reveals her miraculous nature in Rhöides' account by refusing the teat on fast-days; and before cutting her first teeth she manages to learn by heart the Lord's Prayer in three languages. Then, as a teenager and prior to her adoption of male clothing, she emulates St Uncumber and other hirsute saints, in no uncertain manner, by growing a bushy beard when three monks try to force their attentions on her:

Blessing the Virgin from her very heart for so timely an intervention, Joanna sprang up and wagged her long beard like the head of Medusa until the terrified monks ran from the room. [5]

Luckily for Joanna, the beard disappears as quickly as it came, once the danger has passed. John Briley may have got the idea for the rape scene in the film *Pope Joan* from this episode, but how differently he treats it, and how much less impressive is his heroine in consequence.

There is an abundance of wit and racy humour throughout Rhöides' book. After spending seven years as a monk in the Monastery at Fulda, Joanna, accompanied by her lover Frumentius, travels widely and has several dubious encounters along the way, before arriving in Athens. No believer in keeping herself to herself, she numbers 'one abbot, two bishops, and the eparch of Attica' among her indiscretions while there, but soon she grows bored with the settled life and moves on.

Finally reaching Rome, Joanna becomes renowned for her eloquence, speaking 'only of pleasing and useful things—like the great virtue of the Supreme Pontiff'. Naturally such an approach makes her a favourite with Pope Leo IV, and the refreshingly accessible nature of her discourses quickly results in her universal acclaim. In secret, however, she is praying to the Devil for Leo's death, and even sticking pins in a wax doll made in his likeness. When he does die, it is no surprise that Joanna is elected his successor as John VIII, but the celebrations are marked by omens which bode ill for the future. The papal slippers fall off her feet when she tries to put them on, snow falls on Rome in the middle of summer, earthquakes shake Germany, and dead locusts fall on Normandy—this last detail being lifted directly from Petrarch's apocalyptic view of the events.

Nevertheless, Joanna makes an adequate job of ruling the Papal See for two years, providing much 'bread and circuses' and not losing any of her popularity. But the 'old desires' return before too long and, giving way to temptation, she takes a lover. Here Rhöides follows the fifteenth century writers who misinterpreted Martin Polonus and believed that the father of Pope Joan's child was not the companion of her youth. Frumentius having been left in Athens, the new inamorato is a beautiful young cardinal named Florus, who is the son, or so-called 'nephew', of Leo IV. The inevitable happens and Joanna discovers herself to be pregnant; at which point the author turns to Stephan Blanck's version of the fable (*c.*1500) for the angel who appears to her and offers a choice between disgrace on earth and eternal hell-fire. Choosing the former, the pope dies at the hands of the Roman mob after the birth of her son, and to the accompaniment of another plague of Petrarch's locusts. Her soul is taken off by the angel of her vision, either to Heaven or more likely to Purgatory, but not before the denizens of Hell have put up a spirited, though ultimately unsuccessful, fight in defence of their claim to it.

Two things soon become clear to the sympathetic reader of Rhöides' book: firstly that he researched his subject with more thoroughness than a good many non-fiction writers, and secondly that he was totally besotted with Pope Joan. It is not difficult to share his affection, at least for the image of her which he creates. His characterization of a woman who enjoys in equal measure the search for knowledge and the sins of the flesh is beautifully drawn.

Rhöides cannot possibly have realized how popular his work would become, and what an effect it would have on future novelists who chose Pope Joan as their subject. It directly inspired two more books based on the legend and influenced several others, the most obvious imitation being *The Book of Joanna* (1947) by George Borodin (the pen-name of a surgeon, George Sava), which takes the form of an autobiography by Joanna herself, written in 'the darkest corner of the ninety-ninth grotto of Hell' at the request of God in 1472. His conclave of saints, it seems, had one of their occasional meetings in that year to 'see that the fires of Hell burn not with injustice, but rather that only wickedness is punished', and apparently Joanna was a particular problem to them. In her case, the questions they were required to answer centred not merely on whether she deserved her place in Hell, but also on whether she had ever actually existed.

After the main narrative the scene moves to the Heavenly Court, where a number of witnesses are called before the conclave, including John Hus who offers a very good argument in favour of the ordination of women, and Hippocrates, the tribunal's medical expert, who deals with Joanna's mental and physical state. Eventually, against all the evidence presented to the court, the decision is taken that Joanna never lived at all, and her soul is set free into eternity. The judgement, however, seems to be based less on the facts—which are given in a very mangled and slanted fashion—than on the conclave's inability to accept that a woman could ever have achieved such power. God, on the other hand, is surprisingly approving of Joanna, making remarks like: 'I do not know in what part of my Holy Scriptures it is ordained that the Pope shall be a man, and none but a man.'

All of this is quite original and rather quaint, but the narrative section of the book owes a great deal to Rhöides, even copying the invented names of some of his characters such as Frumentius (who becomes Frumence) and Florus. It follows the earlier version closely until near the end when, instead of succumbing to Cardinal Florus' undoubted charms and becoming pregnant, Joanna is struck down by an illness which causes her stomach to swell, and which is later diagnosed by Hippocrates as a tumour of the uterus. While blessing the crowd in front of St John Lateran, she falls to the ground, haemorrhaging badly, and her sex is discovered by those who rush to minister aid. Why Borodin should have so amended the final part of the tale, going against all the earliest accounts, is hard to understand unless it was that he could not resist bringing his medical knowledge to bear on the matter. There is even less excuse for his toning down of Rhöides' more bawdy scenes, which lose much of their snappy humour in the process.

One or two episodes in *The Book of Joanna* have their origins in a different source; a pleasant novel by Richard Ince entitled *When Joan Was Pope* (1931). This is partly a less racy adaptation of Rhöides, but it has many attractive features and new twists of plot of its own. Joan is portrayed sympathetically as a serious-minded and determined seeker after truth, who enters a monastery to find 'the meaning of life and of death', little realizing that she will also find a lover there. The account presents itself as deriving from a manuscript called *Disquisitio historica de Johanna, Papa Foemins docta Graecis Literis* by 'Nicephorus, monk and mystic of Monte Cassino'. Of course this work, which was supposedly found 'amongst mouldering piles of wallpaper and pots of hardened paint flung aside by the builders' in the cellar of a library on Barra in the Outer Hebrides, is purely imaginary.

Ince's story is distinctive in having some decidedly and delightfully pagan elements. At one point Joan and her lover Brother Escobard, while travelling from Fulda to Athens, stay near Nicomedia at a ruined villa which was formerly the property of the Emperor Julian the Apostate. This provides the setting for a lengthy interlude during which our heroine encounters the Great God Pan, who teaches her much about life and the Old Religion, in such a manner that the book almost turns into a paean to paganism as we see its purity contrasted with the decadence of the Church.

In Rome, Joan is sickened by the sale of saints' bones which she observes in the streets, and by the barbarism and narrow-mindedness of the clergy, so she makes it her object to 'convince the barbarians of her day that wisdom had walked the earth long ere the coming of Christianity'. Her lectures on the early Greek philosophers and writers become very fashionable, but her attacks on corruption within the Church naturally make her some influential enemies, who spread rumours that she is a heretic, a black magician, the Antichrist or even a woman. They do not, of course, realize the truth of this last accusation at the time, and are therefore unable to prevent her from becoming pope when Leo IV dies. In fact, Ince's Joan has no real desire for the position and power, which are offered to her solely for political reasons, but she decides to accept the pontificate in order to initiate some long-needed reforms within the Church. Perhaps she sets about her task a little too zealously though, for she continues to make enemies, including a certain Demetria, 'Countess of Trebbia and Senatrix of the City of Rome'; the most formidable secular woman in the city, who cannot understand why Joan so easily resists her feminine wiles.

In the end, Cardinal Lambert of Salerno, a close friend of the pope, is kidnapped by the enemy faction led by the Lady Demetria and the unpleasant Cardinal Malcolm. While Joan's troops are occupied in rescuing him, she herself is killed by a mob which has been stirred up against her. Immediately the malicious slander of her death in childbirth is invented, and gossips spread the story that 'She was overcome with the pains of childbirth . . . and gave birth to a boy. Fortunately he died, for he must have been Antichrist . . . it had the number 666 branded in white on either palm'.[6] No doubt Ince had been reading Sabine Baring-Gould!

The book's witty but slightly inaccurate introduction makes it clear that Ince's sympathies lay with Joan, whom he saw as a real woman unjustly treated: 'Many a Pope became a father . . . and nothing was said, but immediately that Joan becomes a mother the voice of scandal cries to heaven'.

Similar sentiments are expressed more vehemently in Clement Wood's *The Woman Who Was Pope*, which was published in the same year as Ince's fantasy. The non-fiction introduction is an intensely anti-Catholic diatribe distinguished only by its use of the most startlingly labyrinthine logic, but most of the work is devoted to a fictional portrayal of the female pope, which does make marginally better reading. The author calls it an 'interpretative' biography, meaning in practice that it is as much a product of the imagination as all the other modern novels about Pope Joan. This is so despite a forlorn attempt to create an authentic historical background.

Wood appears to have taken the bare outline of his narrative from earlier novelists, but his version is very different from theirs in the telling. The obligatory journey from Fulda to Rome in the company of her first lover (here called Cenwulf) is undertaken, but it brings Joan to England and Paris as well as to Athens. Curiously, when she reaches Rome, her new lover and the father of her child proves to be the humble young Father Adrian, who goes on to become the unquestionably historical Pope Hadrian II (867–72), famous for the extreme reluctance with which he accepted the papal crown. At this point, and not for the first time, the book's much-vaunted accuracy collapses, for the real Hadrian was about sixty years old in 855, and already had a wife and daughter, who were later to meet a sorry end at the hands of a relative of Anastasius the Librarian.

Clement Wood's biggest error of judgement is his decision to exclude almost all supernatural episodes from Joan's biography. His story only comes to life at one point towards the end, when the betraying demon from the thirteenth century *Flores Temporum* puts in an appearance in the body of a demoniac. Shortly afterwards, Stephan Blanck's angel offers the usual means to salvation, and the inevitable choice is made. Aside from these paranormal events we are mostly treated to a procession of detailed descriptions of the various disputations and discourses for which Joan becomes famous in the course of her travels. Sometimes they are humorously told, but on the whole they make a poor substitute for the zest and vigour of Rhöides and Ince.

Although sharing the same, unoriginal title as Rhöides' masterpiece, Renée Dunan's *Pope Joan*, the English translation of which was published in 1930, is definitely not to be confused with it. Indeed, Dunan's account of 'Joanna, child of chance, monk, soldier, beggar, brigand, prostitute, wife of pashas, camel-woman, philosopher, evangelist and Pope' has very little in common with any other version of the legend. The list of Joanna's successive occupations makes the book sound extremely exciting, but the reader who expects something for all tastes is doomed to disappointment. The tale fails throughout, because of the tediously melodramatic way in which it is related. The almost compulsory non-fiction introduction is no better, resting as it does on the assumption that the woman pontiff did exist, but that all the contemporary documents which might have provided the necessary evidence were deliberately destroyed. We have already discussed this tiresomely paranoid theory and found it wanting.

'In the large room of a house in a certain quiet city in Flanders, a man was gilding a devil': such is the atmospheric opening of a novel about a female pope who, for a change, is definitely not Pope Joan. *Black Magic*, subtitled 'A Tale of the Rise and Fall of the Antichrist', was written by the popular author Marjorie Bowen, and first appeared in print in 1909. Freed from the constraints of the traditional story, Bowen was able to produce a thoroughly original work. It revolves around a nun, Ursula of Rooselaare, who takes on the disguise of a man and becomes a scholar of some distinction, specializing in the magical arts. After being forced to flee first from Basle University and then from Frankfurt when her sorceries and intrigues are discovered, she adopts the identity of a saintly, recently dead youth named Blaise. Aided by her occult skills and a little blackmail, her rise to power is meteoric, and soon she ascends the papal throne as Michael II, thus becoming not only a female pope but also, for some reason, the Antichrist.

At the peak of her success, and when it seems that nothing can stop her, she loses everything for the love of her long-time (and ever unsuspecting) friend Theirry. 'Pope Michael' almost succeeds in securing the Imperial Crown for him, but his weakness alone brings about her downfall. It is a tribute to Marjorie Bowen's talents that she makes the reader identify totally with Ursula, in spite of her cruelty and heartlessness.

The period in which the tale is set is nowhere explicitly stated, but it would be a mistake to assign it to the usual era of Pope Joan, in the ninth century, even though this is asserted by the anonymous writer of the book's Foreword.[7] In fact the events seem to occur some time around 1200. They can certainly be placed no more than fifty years earlier than that, for Peter Abelard (1079–1142) is mentioned as a great scholar of the past. Needless to say, there has never been a Pope Michael II, nor even a Michael I.

Ursula of Rooselaare's life-story owes nothing to that of the legendary female pope, but this very originality adds to its interest. *Black Magic* is unquestionably a classic of its kind and all the more impressive because Marjorie Bowen was little more than a teenager when she wrote it. Later she went on to produce an enormous range of books and stories; some of which, like the truly memorable ghostly tale 'The Crown Derby Plate', again reached the high standard set by *Black Magic*.

The myth of the woman pontiff has fascinated and intrigued authors and playwrights for almost 500 years, and it still retains its interest today. Apart from the feminist play *Top Girls*—in which Pope Joan does not take a central role— probably her most recent appearance was in a BBC radio play of the late 1970s, where her case was investigated by a modern young woman who found her enquiries unaccountably blocked on all sides. The single remaining medium which has not yet featured Joan is television, but her debut there can only be a matter of time.

8

POPE JOAN AND THE TAROT

JUST one facet of the development of Pope Joan's legend remains to be looked at, but it is important, for above all others it is the one which has made her image familiar to vast numbers of people. However, the Female Pope or High Priestess card in the Tarot pack only appeared some 200 years after the story of Joan first arose, so it cannot have influenced the myth in its formative stages. The card is normally given the number two in the Major Trumps, and card number five, The Pope, is its logical opposite; just as The Empress and The Emperor (three and four respectively) counter-balance one another. The Female Pope is usually portrayed as a seated woman wearing clerical dress and a triple crown, and holding an open book on her lap. A detailed discussion of her particular significance to fortune-tellers and other Tarot card readers would be out of place here. Suffice it to say that she is supposed to represent hidden or esoteric knowledge, which is appropriate enough for a figure like Pope Joan who was noted for her scholarship and, so some writers claimed, her experience in the occult sciences.

The origin and initial purpose of the Tarot is obscure, but there does seem to be a connection between what was probably the earliest Female Pope card to appear in the deck, and a genuine historical event.

Around 1260, a pious and wealthy woman named Guglielma of Bohemia (although she came from England according to one contemporary) arrived in Milan and quickly gained a following as a preacher. When she died in 1281, her body was entombed in the Cistercian house at Chiaravalle near Milan, and—as so often happened in the Middle Ages—a cult grew up around her relics. By the reign of Pope Boniface VIII (1294–1303), Guglielma's more fanatical followers had come to believe that she was the incarnation of the Holy Spirit and would return, to throw down the incumbent pontiff and install a young Milanese woman called Maifreda di Pirovano on the vacant throne. This would inaugurate the Age of the Spirit foretold by Joachim of Fiore, which was by then a little late, having been expected by Joachim's supporters in 1260. The date of Guglielma's return was set for the Pentecost of 1300, and in preparation Maifreda began to celebrate mass among her disciples, while plans were formulated for a new college of cardinals which would consist either entirely or at least partly of women. The ecclesiastical authorities could hardly be expected to look kindly on such a sect, even though it never had more than a couple of hundred members and was no real threat to them. Inevitably Maifreda and several other Guglielmites, both male and female, became victims of the Inquisition and were burned at the stake in 1300. The movement died with them.[1]

Had these events taken place before 1250 it might even be argued that they could have given birth to the entire Pope Joan story, but in fact her legend pre-dates by many years the formation of the Guglielmite sect, which only came properly into being on the death of its eponymous leader. Perhaps the converse may be true. In the Age of the Holy Spirit, which was and still is traditionally thought of as female, it would be perfectly natural to have a woman ruling the Church, but there is no reason why such a woman should have been called pope, which is by definition a male title. It may be that the Guglielmites saw nothing odd in Maifreda being a future pope because they had heard rumours that another member of her sex, albeit in masculine disguise, had already attained the position.

Maifreda, a nun from the convent of the Umiliata Order at Biassono, forms a significant link between the Tarot and the Guglielmites, for she was a relative—probably a cousin—of Matteo Visconti, a member of the great Visconti family. It was this family which, two centuries later, commissioned several decks of Tarot cards. One, the so-called Visconti-Sforza deck attributed to Bonifacio Bembo, was almost certainly the first to include a figure resembling the female pope. Instead of papal vestments she wears a brown monastic garment, but on her wimpled head is the triple crown of the successors of St Peter, while the characteristic book is open on her lap. Unfortunately, like the rest of the pack, her card bears no name, so a positive identification is impossible. Gertrude Moakley, the writer of the definitive book on the Bembo pack, believes she recognizes the nun's habit as belonging to the Umiliata order,[2] and argues therefore that the card represents Maifreda herself; an aspiring rather than a real pontiff.

Clearly the origin of the pack renders this theory not at all unacceptable, but one nondescript brown garment is much like another, and the case is not conclusively proven. There are, after all, several other possible explanations for the artist's inclusion of the un-named, mysterious woman. She may, for instance, be nothing more than a personification of Faith or Charity; two Virtues who often appeared as sombre and dignified females in the early tarocchi decks, which were the forerunners of the Tarot. However, the legend of Pope Joan was at the peak of its popularity in the middle of the fifteenth century when the Visconti-Sforza cards were made, so it remains quite likely that the woman was intended to be Joan herself. Certainly later Tarot-makers assumed this to be so. The earliest known list of the titles of the Major Trumps, which forms part of a sermon against the evils of gambling dating from about 1500, includes 'La Papessa';[3]

and for 200 years most, though not all, decks featured her.

One noteworthy exception was the work of the Catholic designer Giuseppe Maria Mitelli, who—in 1664 at a time when the Catholic Church had acquired a more sceptical attitude to the female pope—was not content merely to cut her out of his tarocchini. Instead, he replaced the normal Pope and Female Pope cards with depictions of a standing and a seated pontiff, both bearded and therefore male, St Uncumber notwithstanding.

By the eighteenth century some Tarot decks had become more classically oriented, and included a card of Juno and her peacock, symbolizing immortality and resurrection, instead of the Female Pope. Juno, and her partner Jupiter on the Pope card, were especially popular in Switzerland and Southern France. The nineteenth century occultists, on the other hand, preferred the original version, but modified in such a way as to be more in keeping with their own beliefs. Many elements from magical symbolism crept in and the card's alternative title, The High Priestess, was increasingly used. To many designers the magical and occult features of the card were of paramount importance and the concept of Pope Joan was almost forgotten. It was probably Oswald Wirth who began the trend with his 'Papesse', whose papal mitre is surmounted by a crescent moon and whose book bears the yin-yang symbol. Wirth's symbolism was embroidered upon by A.E. Waite to the point where, in his enduringly popular pack, the former Female Pope is entirely unrecognizable. His High Priestess sits between the two columns of the Temple, inscribed 'B' and 'J', for Boaz and Jachin. She has a crescent moon at her feet, a scroll of the Torah in her hands, and her head-dress is uncompromisingly pagan.

This tendency to abandon the traditional image in favour of an odd mixture of pagan and Christian elements has continued to the present day, although an occasional modern Tarot still includes a pleasant enough portrayal of Pope Joan.

The woman pontiff's connection with cards does not end with the Tarot, however, for there is also a card game named after her. 'Pope Joan' seems to have derived at some time in the early nineteenth century from a French game called 'The Yellow Dwarf'. In its turn it gave birth to 'Newmarket', and while that game and its variants continue to be played regularly, 'Pope Joan' itself is now but rarely seen. The rules are much like those of 'Newmarket', except that the Nine of Diamonds or 'Pope' card plays an important role. An alternative title for this card is the 'Curse of Scotland', and a number of inventive but rather dubious explanations have been put forward to account for the appellation. None of them is in any way relevant to Pope Joan. In fact, there seems to be no obvious reason why her name should have been attached to the game at all.

AFTERWORD

FROM the middle of the thirteenth century right down to the present day, interest in the Pope Joan legend has never really flagged, although it has been seen in various different lights through the years. The long life of the story must in part reflect its political value to those who wished to malign the papacy, starting with disgruntled members of the mendicant orders within the Catholic Church, and continuing with the Protestants. Nevertheless, we believe it would have survived even without this. There is a universal fascination with tales of women who, for one reason or another, disguise themselves as men. Male transvestism seems inevitably to carry with it the taint of deviant sexuality, whereas females who adopt men's clothing are usually seen as being motivated by nothing more unhealthy than a desire to improve their status in this world or the next. If their imposture is complete and successful then they are treated with respect and sometimes admiration. Thus the cult of St Hildegund, who lived for many months as a Cistercian novice, was very popular in the Middle Ages; as were the histories of legendary female monks such as St Eugenia. Yet an unfortunate eunuch who entered a nunnery in the sixth century, according to Gregory of Tours, was accused of immorality with the nuns and, despite his proven innocence, has come down to us as a far from heroic figure.[1]

More recently the life of the eighteenth century male transvestite, the Chevalier D'Eon, has provoked both ridicule and pity; while much less extreme emotions are roused by the equally odd James Barry, the Scottish army surgeon whose remarkable career spanned four continents and fifty years, and who proved on her death in 1865 to be a woman.

The sin of Joan of Arc appears to have been not so much that she dressed in male attire, as that she maintained a firm female identity while doing so. Similarly, almost all the old writers on Pope Joan agree that her downfall was not caused by her original deception, but by her final lapse into feminine weakness when she became pregnant. To attack the papacy with maximum effect it was not sufficient to invent a woman pope; she also had to be shown as a failed pseudo-man.

We have found some authors who scoff at the whole idea of a female pontiff, for no better reason than that they cannot conceive of a member of the 'second sex' having the wit to reach the supreme position in the Catholic Church unrecognized. For C.A. Patrides, whose recent study adds little new to the subject, the medieval belief in Pope Joan is enough to make him 'suspect that judgment had fled to brutish beasts, and men had lost their reason.'[2] We do not share this extreme view. St Hildegund seems to have entered the monastery at Schönau because it was the easiest and most convenient thing for her to do at the time, but the fact remains that she lived and worked among monks without her secret being revealed. Another woman could well have taken the same step out of unwillingness to accept the traditional supportive, nurturing role which was the only one then available to her within the Church or, indeed, outside it. If she had sufficient determination, what might she not have achieved? It is certainly not impossible that she might finally have gained the ultimate accolade of election to the Papal Chair.

Possible it may be, but as far as we can tell, it never happened; unless of course she was one of the known historical popes, and so perfect was her disguise that she went to her grave undiscovered. That is a wholly different question, and one which may never be answered conclusively.

Appendix

SOURCES FOR
SAINT HILDEGUND

THE earliest source for the story of the woman monk, St Hildegund, is in a manuscript from the monastery of Ebrach, [1] less than one hundred miles north-east of her own abbey at Schönau. There is little reason to doubt the statement in the text, that it was written late in the very year of Hildegund's death; 1188. On internal stylistic evidence it has been attributed to a Cistercian abbot, Engelhard, whose informant is given as an eyewitness 'who was present at the death and burial of the girl and has passed on to us what he heard and saw of her'. Engelhard records that the Abbot of Schönau had commissioned his own investigation and account of the miraculous novice, and that the present 'little study' was intended to suffice only until that one was published. It is not known whether the Abbot's official report was ever completed. None of the sources in existence today would appear to fit its description, though one or more may have been adapted from it.

Nearly as old as the Ebrach manuscript is a Metrical Life of Hildegund which is part of a codex from Windberg, [2] a Premonstratensian monastery near Regensburg (about 170 miles south-east of Schönau). The story it tells is almost identical to Engelhard's, but the use of different language throughout indicates that it is not simply a copy. It is, at any rate, very early, having been written for Abbot Gebehard of Windberg, who died in 1191.

Neither of these earliest accounts give Hildegund's name. Instead they call her Joseph throughout, stating that her own name had not yet been discovered and that, in consequence, she was entered into the monastery's Calendar as 'A hand-maiden of Christ in Schönau'. The first version to provide this missing piece of information comes from a manuscript formerly owned by the College of the Society of Jesus at Paderborn (140 miles north of Schönau). [3] It states that:

When several days had passed after her most holy death, the brothers, wishing to know her name, sent into the area around Cologne where, as she had revealed, she was born. After zealous enquiry, they found a certain old woman who was related to the blessed maid, and from whom they discovered that her name was Hildegund.

The text of this codex probably dates from the first or second decade of the thirteenth century. It was undoubtedly known to Caesar of Heisterbach when he gave his version of events in the *Dialogus Miraculorum*, written in the 1220s and 1230s. [4] That he took the main part of Hildegund's story from the Paderborn manuscript, or at least from a near identical one, is clear since he copied some slight variations which appeared there for the first time. For instance, the two earliest accounts tell how, when Hildegund was hanging from the gibbet, an angel predicted her death exactly three years hence. The Paderborn version gives the period as two years and, sure enough, so does Caesar. However, the fact that Caesar used other written material when telling his story does not necessarily give the lie to his claim that his source was Hermannus, a monk who, at the age of fourteen, had been a fellow novice of Hildegund. Although the narrative of her life, as given in her confession, is copied from elsewhere, the anecdotes of her time in the monastery are completely original to Caesar, and it may have been these alone which he obtained from Hermannus.

Rather later than all of these, though probably still belonging to the first half of the thirteenth century, is a Life of St Hildegund included by the Bollandists in the *Acta Sanctorum*. [5] It is a long and laboured text, filled with biblical quotations, and where it varies from the earlier versions it almost always tends towards the miraculous or the historically inaccurate. For an example of the former we need look no further than Hildegund's birth. There is nothing miraculous about this in the other manuscripts, but the *Acta Sanctorum* insists that she (and her sister Agnes, who here becomes her twin for the first time) was born only as a result of her aged parents' dedication of themselves and their longed-for offspring to God. The wondrous birth of a child to an aged and despairing mother through prayer has, of course, many precedents, the most famous being the story of Samuel; but it is also told of one of the legendary women monks, St Euphrosyne.

The most striking inaccuracy of the *Acta Sanctorum* Life comes when it deals with Hildegund's employment as a letter carrier. In 1183 an election for a new archbishop of Trèves (Trier) took place, but two different candidates were elected to the post, and controversy raged as to whether Rudolf of Wied, former provost of the Cathedral, or Archdeacon Folmar was the rightful new occupant of the bishop's throne. The Emperor and his son took Rudolf's side while Folmar was championed by the Pope and also by Philip, Archbishop of Cologne. The situation lasted for over five years, during which time the Emperor threatened with flogging, or even death, anyone found carrying letters concerning the matter to the Pope. [6] Thus when, in 1185 (or 1186 in the later accounts), Hildegund was commissioned to take letters to the Pope, it was because a young 'man' on foot and disguised as a pilgrim (with the letters hidden in her staff) would be less suspect on the road, and more likely to pass through the Emperor's road-blocks, than an emissary on horseback.

Now, all the accounts from Engelhard's to Caesar's describe how Hildegund went to Verona to see the Pope, whereas the *Acta Sanctorum* states that she only stopped briefly in Verona to meet up with the envoy who had employed her, before going on immediately to Rome where she found the Pope. Here are all the signs of late work, for the Pope was indeed based in Verona throughout the period we are considering. Lucius III arrived in that city on 22 July, 1184, and died there on 25 November, 1185. His successor Urban III was crowned in Verona on 1 December, 1185, and did not leave until a month or so before his death in October 1187.[7] The Papacy was then based in Ferrara and Pisa for a short while before returning to Rome in February 1188, by which time Hildegund had long since completed her mission and become a novice at Schönau.

The *Acta Sanctorum* account is obviously the only one of these five which was written sufficiently long enough after the event for the details of the Papacy's residence in Verona to have been forgotten. Its writer asserts that he was a friend and confidant of Hildegund at Schönau, and adds melodramatically that a vision of the maid two years after her death cured him of a serious illness. While it would be wrong to disregard these claims as certain fiction, the over-dramatic and highly derivative nature of this particular Life rules out an early date and casts grave doubts on it as authentic eye-witness testimony.

BIBLIOGRAPHY

The following abbreviations have been used throughout the bibliography.

MGH:SS   *Monumenta Germaniae Historica: Scriptores*
OC   M. Le Quien, *Oriens Christianus* (1745)
RGSS   *Rerum Germanicarum Scriptores aliquot insignes*, ed. J. Pistorius (1726)
RISS   *Rerum Italicarum Scriptores*, ed. L.A. Muratori
SBI   *Scriptorum Brunsvicensia Illustrantium*, ed. G.G. Leibnitz (1710)

A. *Early Sources*

Adam of Usk, *Chronicon Adae de Usk 1377-1404*, ed. & trans. Edward Maunde Thompson (1876).
Bellarmine, Robert, *De Summo Pontifice; Opera Omnia* (1872), I, pp.474–5.
Boccaccio, Giovanni, *Concerning Famous Women*, trans. Guido A. Guarino (1964), _____, *De Mulieribus Claris* (1539).
Brewyn, William, *A XVth Century Guide-Book to the Principal Churches of Rome*, trans. C. Eveleigh Woodruff (1933).
Burchard, John, *Liber Notarum*; *RISS*, XXXII pt 1, vol 1, pp.83, 176.
Capgrave, John, *Ye Solace of Pilgrimes. A Description of Rome, circa AD 1450*, ed. C.A. Mills & H.M. Bannister (1911).
Chronica Minor Auctore Minorita Erphordiensi; *MGH:SS*, XXIV, p.184.
Chronicon Salernitanum; *MGH:SS*, III, p.481.
Erchempert, *Historia Langobardorum Beneventi degentium*; *RISS*, V, p.32.
Eulogium, Chronicon ab orbe condito usque ad annum 1366, ed. Frank Scott Haydon (1858).
Flores Historiarum; *Rolls Series* I (1890), ed. H.R. Luard, p.425.
Flores Temporum Auctore Fratre Ordinis Minorum: Pontifices; *MGH:SS*, XXIV, p.243.
Gaufridus de Collone, *Chronicon*; *MGH:SS*, XXVI, p.615.
Gotfrid of Viterbo, *Pantheon*; *RGSS*, II, p.372.
Haemerlein, Felix, *De Nobilitate et Rusticitate Dialogus* (circa 1490).
Hasenmuller, Elias, *Historia Iesuitici Ordinis* (1593).
Higden, Ranulph, *Polycronycon* (1527 reprint).

Historia Erphesfordensis Anonymi Scriptoris De Landgraviis Thuringiae; RGSS, I, p.1302.

Jean de Mailly, *Chronica Universalis Mettensis*; MGH:SS, XXIV, p.514.

Marianus Scotus, *Historiographi sui temporis clarissimi*; RGSS, I, p.639.

Martin Polonus, *Chronicon Pontificum et Imperatum*; MGH:SS, XXII, p.428.

Mirabilia Urbis Romae. The Marvels of Rome; or A Picture of the Golden City, ed. Francis Morgan Nichols (1889).

Petrarch, Franceso, *Chronica de le Vite de Pontefici et Imperadori Romani* (1534).

Rolevinck, Werner, *Fasciculus Temporum omnes antiquorum chronicas complectens*; RGSS, II, p.528

Schedel, Hartmannus, *Liber Chronicarum* (1493).

Sigebert of Gemblours, *Chronographia*; RGSS, I, p.794.

Stephen of Bourbon, *De Diversis Materiis Praedicabilibus; Scriptores Ordinis Praedicatorum*, J. Quetif & J. Echard, I (1719), p.367.

Theodoric Engelhusius, *Chronicon*; SBI, II, p.1065.

Tiraqueau, André, *De Legibus Connubialibus, et Iure Maritali; Opera Omnia* (1597), II, p.188.

William of Ockham, *Opus Nonaginta Dierum; Opera Politica*, ed. J.G. Sikes & H.S. Offler (1963), II, p.854.

Wolfius, John, *Lectionum Memorabilium et Reconditarum Centenarii XVI* (1671), I, p.231 (Stephan Blanck), p.230 (Baptista Mantuanus).

B. *Religious Polemic*

Cooke, Alexander, *Pope Joane. A Dialogue Between a Protestant and A Papist* (1610).

Cope, Alan, *Dialogi Sex Contra Pontificatos* (1566).

Francklin, John Fairfax, and Clement, William, *The Vicar of Whaplode and 'Pope Joan'* (1876).

Harding, Thomas, *A Confutation of a Booke Intituled An Apologie of the Church of England* (1565, facsimile reprint 1976).

History of Pope Joan and the Whores of Rome, The (1687).

H.S., *Historia De Donne Famose or The Romaine Iubile which happened in the yeare 855* (English translation 1599).

I.M., *The Anatomie of Pope Ioane* (1624).

Jewel, John, *Defence of the Apology of the Church of England; The Works of John Jewel*, Parker Society, IV (1850), pp.648–56.

Poulson, Edward, *The End of the Papacy* (1901).

A Present for a Papist, ed. with additions by H. Shuttleworth (1785).

R.W., *Pope Joan, or an Account collected out of the Romish Authors . . .* (1689).

C. *Secondary Sources*

Adinolfi, Pasquale, *Roma nell'età di Mezzo* (1881), I.

Baring-Gould, Sabine, *Curious Myths of the Middle Ages* (1877 reprint).

Bayle, Pierre, *Dictionary* (1710).

Bumpus, T.F., *The Cathedrals and Churches of Italy* (1926).

Davis, Elizabeth Gould, *The First Sex* (1973).

Döllinger, John J.I., Von, *Fables Respecting the Popes of the Middle Ages*, trans. Alfred Plummer (1871).

D'Onofrio, Cesare, *La Papessa Giovanna: Roma E Papato Tra Storia E Leggenda* (1979).

Duchesne, Louis, *Étude sur le 'Liber Pontificalis'* (1886).

Fuller, Graham, and Knight, Ian, 'The Lady is a Pope?'; *The Unexplained*, XIII, no.151 (1983), pp.3014–17.

L'Enfant, James, *The History of the Council of Constance*, trans. S. Whatley (1730).

Le Quien, M., *Oriens Christianus* (1745).

Mosheim, John Laurence, *Ecclesiastical History*, trans. Archibald Maclaine (1826), II.

Müntz, Eugène, 'La Légende de la Papesse Jeanne dans l'illustration des Livres, du XVe au XIXe siècle'; *La Bibliofilia*, (1900) pt 2, pp.325–39.

Patrides, C.A., *Premises and Motifs in Renaissance Thought and Literature* (1982).

Perrodo-Le Moyne, Henri, *Un Pape Nommé Jeanne* (1972).

Rhöides, Emmanuel D., *Pope Joan—A Historical Study* (1886).

Thurston, Herbert, *Pope Joan* (1929 reprint).

Tomassetti, G., 'La Statua Della Papessa Giovanna'; *Bullettino Della Commissione Archeologica Comunale de Roma*, XXXV (1907), pp.82–95.

D. *Drama, Fiction and the Tarot*

Borodin, George, *The Book of Joanna* (1947).

Bowen, Marjorie, *Black Magic* (1974 reprint).

Dunan, Renée, *Pope Joan*, trans. Hélène Graeme (1930).

Fauconpret, C., *La Papesse Jeanne: Opéra-Bouffon en Vaudevilles, en Trois Actes* (1793).

Ince, Richard, *When Joan was Pope* (1931).

Innes, Brian, *The Tarot: How to use and interpret the cards* (1977).

Kaplan, Stuart R., *The Encyclopedia of Tarot*, I (1978).

Moakley, Gertrude, *The Tarot Cards Painted by Bonifacio Bembo* (1966).

Rhöides, Emmanuel D., *Pope Joan: A Romantic Biography*, trans. Lawrence Durrell (1960 reprint).

Settle, Elkanah, *The Female Prelate: being the history of the life and death of Pope Joan* (1680).

Schernberg, Dietrich, *Ein Schön Spiel von Frau Jutten* (1971 reprint).

Schröder, Edward, 'Goethe's Faust und "Das Spiel von Frau Jutten"'; *Vierteljahrschrift für Litteraturgeschichte* (1891) pt 4, pp.336–9.

Wood, Clement, *The Woman Who Was Pope* (1931).

E. *Female Monks and Other Saints*

Anson, John, 'The Female Transvestite in Early Monasticism: The Origin and

Development of a Motif'; *Viator*, V (1974), pp.1–32.

Bullough, Vern L., 'Transvestites in the Middle Ages'; *American Journal of Sociology*, LXXIX pt 6, pp.1381–94.

Butler's Lives of the Saints, Thurston and Attwater edition (1956).

'De B. Hugolina Virgine'; *Acta Sanctorum* (1867 reprint), August (ii), pp.395–8.

Delcourt, Marie, *Hermaphrodite: Myths and Rites of the Bisexual Figure in Classical Antiquity*, trans. Jennifer Nicholson (1961).

Delehaye, Hippolyte, *The Legends of the Saints*, trans. Mrs V.M. Crawford (1974 reprint).

Dunbar, Agnes B.C., *A Dictionary of Saintly Women* (1904).

James, M.R., *The Apocryphal New Testament* (1924) ('The Acts of Paul and Thecla').

Lacey, J. Hubert, 'Anorexia Nervosa and a Bearded Female Saint'; *British Medical Journal*, CCLXXXV (18–25 December 1982), pp.1816–17.

O'Leary, De Lacy, *The Saints of Egypt* (1937).

Select Narratives of Holy Women, trans. Agnes Smith Lewis; *Studia Sinaitica* 10 (1900) (St Eugenia and St Euphrosyne).

Three Coptic Legends: Hilaria, Archellites, The Seven Sleepers, ed. & trans. James Drescher, *Supplément aux Annales Du Service des Antiquités de L'Égypte*, IV (1947).

Thurston, Herbert, 'The Story of St Hildegund, Maiden and Monk'; *The Month*, February 1916, pp.145–56.

Waddell, Helen, *The Desert Fathers* (1936) ('The Life of St Pelagia the Harlot').

Warner, Marina, *Joan of Arc: The Image of Female Heroism* (1981).

For St Hildegund see also *Notes and References (Appendix)*

NOTES AND REFERENCES

THE FOLLOWING abbreviations have been used throughout this section.

MGH:SS   *Monumenta Germaniae Historica: Scriptores*
OC   M. Le Quien, *Oriens Christianus* (1745)
RGSS   *Rerum Germanicarum Scriptores aliquot insignes*, ed. J. Pistorius (1726)
RISS   *Rerum Italicarum Scriptores*, ed. L.A. Muratori
SBI   *Scriptorum Brunsvicensia Illustrantium*, ed. G.G. Leibnitz (1710)

To avoid irritation and confusion, all the quotations from the sources listed below are to be found translated into English throughout the text.

1: THE EARLIEST APPEARANCES OF POPE JOAN

1. Martin Polonus, *Chron. Pont. et Imp.*; *MGH:SS*, XXII, p.428.
2. Vatican MS 3762. See Louis Duchesne, *Étude sur le 'Liber Pontificalis'* (1886), p.95. A facsimile of the page in question appears in H. Perrodo-Le Moyne, *Un Pape Nommé Jeanne* (1972).
3. Anastasius, *Lib. Pont.*, quoted in *OC*, III, col. 394.
4. Alexander Cooke, *Pope Joane* (1610).
5. Marianus Scotus, *Hist. sui temp. clar.*; *RGSS*, I, p.639.
6. Pistorius' notes on Marianus; *RGSS*, I, p.794.
7. *Hist. sui temp. clar.*; *MGH:SS*, VIII, p.550.
8. Sigebert of Gemblours, *Chron.*; *RGSS*, I, p.794.
9. Gotfrid of Viterbo, *Pantheon*; *RGSS*, II, p.372.
10. Gotfrid, *Speculum Regum*; *MGH:SS*, XXII, pp.29–30.
11. Jean de Mailly, *Chron. Univ. Mett.*; *MGH:SS*, XXIV, p.514. In the original Latin, Joan is referred to in the masculine gender, but we have altered this for ease of reading.
12. Stephen of Bourbon, *De Div. Mat. Praed.*; *Scriptores Ordinis Praedicatorum*, I (1719), p.367.
13. John J. I. Von Döllinger, *Fables Respecting the Popes of the Middle Ages* (1871), p.44.
14. *Chron. Minor*; *MGH:SS*, XXIV, p.184.
15. *Flores Temp.*; *MGH:SS*, XXIV, p.243.
16. Felix Haemerlein, *De Nobil. et Rust. Dial.* (*c*.1490), f.99.

17. Giovanni Boccaccio, *De Mulieribus Claris* (1539), f.63.
18. Döllinger, op. cit., p.64.
19. Theodoric Engelhusius, *Chron.*; *SBI*, II, p.1065.
20. *OC*, III, col.386.
21. *Flores Hist.*; *Rolls Series* I (1890), p.425.
22. *OC*, III, col.381.
23. Werner Rolevinck, *Fasc. Temp.*; *RGSS*, II, p.528.
24. *Hist. Erphesford.*; *RGSS*, I, p.1302.

2: LATER SOURCES

1. Ranulph Higden, *Polycronycon* (1527), bk 5, f.226.
2. Quoted in John Jewel, *Defence of the Apology; The Works of John Jewel*, IV (1850), p.648.
3. Giovanni Boccaccio, *De Mulieribus Claris* (1539), f.63, and *Concerning Famous Women* (1964), p.231.
4. Adam of Usk, *Chron. Adae de Usk* (1876), pp.88, 215. For John Hus see James L'Enfant, *The History of the Council of Constance* (1730), I, p.340.
5. John J. I. Von Döllinger, *Fables Respecting the Popes of the Middle Ages* (1871), Appendix B, pp.280–2.
6. Boccaccio, op. cit., f.63, and pp.232–3.
7. *Eulogium, Chron.* (1858), p.243.
8. Martin Polonus, *Chron. Pont. et Imp.*; *MGH:SS*, XXII, p.428.
9. *Mirabilia Urbis Romae* (1889), pp.139–40.
10. Quotation and illustration appear in John Wolfius, *Lect. Mem. et Recond. Cent. XVI* (1671), I, p.230.
11. Felix Haemerlein, *De Nobil. et Rust. Dial.* (*c.*1490), f.99.
12. Wolfius, op. cit., I, p.231.
13. Franceso Petrarch, *Chron. de le Vite de Pont. et Imp.* (1534), p.72.
14. *Mirabilia Urbis Romae* (1889), pp.139–40.
15. Adam of Usk, op. cit., pp.88, 215.
16. John Capgrave, *Ye Solace of Pilgrimes* (1911), p.74.
17. See Emmanuel D. Rhöides, *Pope Joan—A Historical Study* (1886), p.82.
18. Wolfius, op. cit., I, p.231.
19. Pasquale Adinolfi, *Roma nell'età de Mezzo* (1881), I, pp.318–19.
20. Döllinger, op. cit., pp.49–50.
21. Gaufridus de Collone, *Chron.*; *MGH:SS*, XXVI, p.615.
22. William Brewyn, *A XVth Century Guide-Book to the Principal Churches of Rome* (1933), p.33.
23. Capgrave, op. cit.
24. See Eugène Müntz, 'La Légende de la Papesse Jeanne . . .'; *La Bibliofilia*, (1900) pt 2, p.330.
25. Hartmannus Schedel, *Liber Chronicarum* (1493), f.169.
26. Haemerlein, op. cit.
27. Döllinger, op. cit., p.34.

28. H.S., *Historia De Donne Famose or The Romaine Iubile which happened in the yeare 855* (Eng. trans. 1599), C2v.
29. André Tiraqueau, *Opera Omnia* (1597), II, p.188.
30. *OC*, III, col.392.
31. William of Ockham, *Opera Politica* (1963), II, p.854.
32. James L'Enfant, op. cit.

3: DID JOAN EXIST?

1. J.D. Mansi, *Sacrorum Conciliorum Amplissima Collectio* (1759), XV, cols 113–19.
2. ibid, XIV, cols 1017–21.
3. *OC*, III, cols 394–5, and Peter Llewellyn, *Rome in the Dark Ages* (1970), p.270.
4. Horace K. Mann, *The Lives of the Popes in the Middle Ages* (1925), II, pp.327–8.
5. *OC*, III, cols 405–6.
6. ibid, III, cols 411–12.
7. ibid, III, col.413.
8. ibid, III, col.423.
9. John Burchard, *Liber Notarum*; *RISS*, XXXII pt 1, vol.1, p.176.
10. J.C. Von Orelli, *Inscriptionum Latinarum Selectarum Amplissima Collectio et Illustrandam Romanae Antiquitatis* (1828), I, pp.407–8.
11. ibid, I, p.409.
12. Eugène Müntz, 'La Légende de la Papesse Jeanne . . .'; *La Bibliofilia*, (1900) pt 2, p.333.
13. Emmanuel D. Rhöides, *Pope Joan—A Historical Study* (1886), p.82.
14. G. Tomassetti, 'La Statua Della Papessa Giovanna'; *Bullettino Della Commissione Archeologica Comunale de Roma*, XXXV (1907), pp.82–95.
15. Robert Bellarmine, *Opera Omnia* (1872), I, pp.474–5.
16. Elias Hasenmuller, *Historia Iesuitici Ordinis* (1593), p.315.
17. Thomas Harding, *A Confutation of a Booke Intituled An Apologie of the Church of England* (1565, facsimile reprint 1976), p.167a;
18. Burchard, op. cit., p.83.
19. Cesare D'Onofrio, *La Papessa Giovanna: Roma E Papato Tra Storia E Leggenda* (1979), figs 85, 86.
20. Müntz, op. cit., pp.330–31.
21. Burchard, op. cit., p.83.
22. Georgina Masson, *The Companion Guide to Rome* (1980), pp.274–5.
23. John J. I. Von Döllinger, *Fables Respecting the Popes of the Middle Ages* (1871), p.50.

4: THEORIES AND FACTS

1. Cesare D'Onofrio, *La Papessa Giovanna: Roma E Papato Tra Storia E Leggenda* (1979), p.206.
2. See John J.I. Von Döllinger, *Fables Respecting the Popes of the Middle Ages* (1871), p.3.
3. Eugène Müntz, 'La Légende de la Papesse Jeanne . . .'; *La Bibliofilia*, (1900) pt 2, p.330.
4. Sabine Baring-Gould, *Curious Myths of the Middle Ages* (1877), p.187.
5. Graham Fuller and Ian Knight, 'The Lady is a Pope?'; *The Unexplained*, XIII, no.151 (1983), p.3017.

6. *The Works of Liudprand of Cremona*, trans. F.A. Wright (1930), p.92.
7. See, for instance, Peter Llewellyn, *Rome in the Dark Ages* (1970).
8. *OC*, III, cols 430–31.
9. *Chron. Salernitanum: MGH:SS*, III, p.481.
10. Erchempert, *Hist. Langobard. Bene. deg.*; *RISS*, V, p.32.
11. *OC*, I, cols 238–9.
12. Much of the basic information about the legendary female monks has been taken from Agnes B.C. Dunbar, *A Dictionary of Saintly Women*, I (1904), and John Anson, 'The Female Transvestite in Early Monasticism: The Origin and Development of a Motif'; *Viator*, V (1974), pp.1–32.
13. Helen Waddell, *The Desert Fathers* (1936), pp.173–88.
14. The quotations concerning St Hildegund are from Caesar of Heisterbach, *Dialogue of Miracles*, trans. G.G. Coulton and Eileen Power (1929), I, pp.51–7. See also Herbert Thurston, 'The Story of St Hildegund, Maiden and Monk'; *The Month*, February 1916, pp.145–56.
15. *Three Coptic Legends: Hilaria, Archellites, The Seven Sleepers*, ed. & trans. James Drescher, *Supplément aux Annales Du Service des Antiquités de L'Egypte*, IV (1947), p.75.
16. 'De B. Hugolina Virgine', *Acta Sanctorum* (1867 reprint), August (ii), pp.395–8.

5: SCEPTICISM AND POLEMIC

1. *OC*, III, col 446.
2. Eugène Müntz, 'La Légende de la Papesse Jeanne . . .'; *La Bibliofilia*, (1900) pt 2, p.331.
3. John Jewel, *Defence of the Apology; The Works of John Jewel*, IV (1850), pp.651, 655.
4. Emmanuel D. Rhöides, *Pope Joan—A Historical Study* (1886), p.51.
5. Jewel, op. cit., p.656.
6. Alan Cope, *Dialogi Sex Contra Summi Pontificatos* (1566), p.47.
7. I.M., *The Anatomie of Pope Ioane* (1624), chap. 3.
8. *The History of Pope Joan and the Whores of Rome* (1687), chap. 1, pt 4.
9. Graham Fuller and Ian Knight, 'The Lady is a Pope?'; *The Unexplained*, XIII, no. 151 (1983), p.3015, and *A Present for a Papist* (1785).
10. M.R. James, *Abbeys* (1926), pp.14–16.
11. Edward Poulson, *The End of the Papacy* (1901), p.62.
12. William of Ockham, *Opera Politica* (1963), II, p.854.

6: MODERN TIMES

1. Pierre Bayle, *Dictionary* (1710), I, p.636.
2. Clement Wood, *The Woman Who Was Pope* (1931), p.34.
3. John Laurence Mosheim, *Ecclesiastical History* (1826), II, pp.270–72.
4. John J.I. Von Döllinger, *Fables Respecting the Popes of the Middle Ages* (1871), p.14.
5. Sabine Baring-Gould, *Curious Myths of the Middle Ages* (1877), pp.161–89.
6. Emmanuel D. Rhöides, *Pope Joan—A Historical Study* (1886), p.90.
7. Henri Perrodo-Le Moyne, *Un Pape Nommé Jeanne* (1972), p.175.
8. Elizabeth Gould Davis, *The First Sex* (1973), pp.267–70.
9. Wood, op. cit., p.65.

10. William of Malmesbury, *Gesta Reg. Angl.*; *Rolls Series* XC pt 1 (Kraus reprint 1964), ed. William Stubbs, p.193.
11. Martin Polonus, *Chron. Pont. et Imp.*; *MGH:SS*, XXII, p.432.
12. So called in *OC*, III, cols 453–4.
13. Horace K. Mann, *The Lives of the Popes in the Middle Ages* (1925), IV, p.331.
14. Sabine Baring-Gould, *A Book of Ghosts* (1904).
15. Carol Riddell, *Divided Sisterhood* (1980), p.18.

7: THE FICTIONAL JOAN

1. Edward Schröder, 'Goethe's Faust und "Das Spiel Von Frau Jutten"'; *Vierteljahrschrift für Litteraturgeschichte* (1891) pt 4, pp.336–39.
2. *Henslowe's Diary*, ed. Walter W. Greg (1908); I, p.13.
3. Elkanah Settle, *The Female Prelate* (1680), Act 5, Scene 4.
4. C. Fauconpret, *La Papesse Jeanne* (1793), Act 3, Scene 4.
5. Emmanuel D. Rhöides, *Pope Joan: A Romantic Biography* (1960), p.44.
6. Richard Ince, *When Joan was Pope* (1931), p.261.
7. Marjorie Bowen, *Black Magic* (1974), p.9.

8: POPE JOAN AND THE TAROT

1. Henry Charles Lea, *A History of the Inquisition of the Middle Ages* (1888), III, pp.90–102.
2. Gertrude Moakley, *The Tarot Cards Painted by Bonifacio Bembo* (1966), pp.72–3.
3. The relevant page from the *Sermones de Ludo Cum Aliis* is reproduced in Stuart R. Kaplan's *The Encyclopedia of Tarot*, I (1978), facing p.1.

AFTERWORD

1. Vern L. Bullough, 'Transvestites in the Middle Ages'; *American Journal of Sociology* LXXIX pt 6, p.1384.
2. C.A.Patrides, *Premises and Motifs in Renaissance Thought and Literature* (1982), p.152.

Appendix: SOURCES FOR SAINT HILDEGUND

1. *Neues Archiv*, VI, pp.515–23.
2. 'Vita Hildegundis Metrica'; *Neues Archiv*, VI, pp.533–6. For the dedication of this manuscript to Abbot Gebehard, see *MGH:SS*, XVII, p.559 note 5.
3. 'De Sancta Hildegunde Virgine'; *Analecta Bollandiana*, VI (1887), Appendix— Catalogue of Brussels Manuscripts pt ii, pp.92–5.
4. Caesar of Heisterbach, *Dialogue of Miracles*, trans. G.G. Coulton and Eileen Power (1929), I, pp.51–7, and *Dialogus Miraculorum*, ed. Joseph Strange (1851), pp.47–53.
5. 'De S. Hildegunde Virgine', *Acta Sanctorum* (1865 reprint), April (ii), pp.778–88.
6. *Cambridge Medieval History*, V (1926), pp.407–9, and Horace K. Mann, *The Lives of the Popes in the Middle Ages* (1925), X, pp.249–53.
7. Philipp Jaffé, *Regesta Pontificum Romanorum* (1851), pp.846–65.

INDEX

Note
Apart from anonymous works
which are listed under title, all
references to chronicles, books, etc,
are indexed under their author.

Abbas Urspergensis, 25
Acta Sanctorum, St Hildegund in,
99–100
Acts of Paul, 61
Adam of Usk, 25, 27, 30, 31, 32,
46
Ademarus of Paris, 25
Adinolfi, Pasquale, 31
Ado, Bishop of Vienna, 40
Alberic, son of Marozia, 55
Albert, antipope, 42
Alexander VI, Pope, 31, 33
Amalric Augerii, 21
Anastasia Patricia, St, 60
Anastasius the Librarian, 12–14,
38–9, 53, 68, 79
Anatomie of Pope Ioane ('I.M.'),
66–7
Anderson, Michael, 86
Annonius of Paris, 25
Antichrist, 35, 54, 59, 91
Pope Joan's son as, 74, 90
Apollinaria (Hilaria), St, 60, 63
Arichis, Duke of Benevento, 57, 58

Baigent, Leigh and Lincoln, 80
Banck, Lawrence, 51
Baring-Gould, Sabine, 54, 74, 81,
90
Baronius, Cardinal, 35, 54, 65, 70
Barry, James, 96
Bayle, Pierre, 72
Bellarmine, Robert, St, 48
Bembo, Bonifacio, 94
Benedict III, Pope, 12, 14, 33,
38–40, 47, 53
Benedict VIII, Pope, 55
Benedict IX, Pope, 55
Berengar, King of Italy, 55
Blanck, Stephan, 29, 31, 88, 91
Blondel, David, 72–3
Boccaccio, Giovanni, 20, 25–6, 29, 43

Bodleian Library, Oxford,
manuscripts at, 21
Boniface VII, antipope, 81
Borodin, George, 88–9
Bowen, Marjorie, 91–2
Brewyn, William, 32, 33
Briley, John, 86, 87
Bumpus, T.F., 35
Burchard, John, 31, 43–4, 47, 49,
53

Caesar of Heisterbach, 62, 63, 99
Capgrave, John, 30, 31, 32
Carvajalius, Joannes, 64
Chesterton, G.K., 75
Chronica Minor, 18–19, 21, 26, 45,
58, 59
Chronicon Salernitanum, 57, 58
Churchill, Caryl, 83, 92
Clement VIII, Pope, 35, 64, 76, 79
Clement, III, antipope, 41–2
Clement, William, 70
Constance, Council of, 26, 36, 80
Constantine, Emperor, 43
Constantinople, female Patriarch of,
56–8
Cooke, Alexander, 14, 68
Cope, Alan, 66, 67

Davis, Elizabeth Gould, 76, 79–82
D'Eon, Chevalier, 96
Döllinger, John J.I. Von, 73–4
Dominic de Guzman, St, 59
Dominicans, 58, 59
D'Onofrio, Cesare, 49–50, 53
Dunan, Renée, 91
Durrell, Lawrence, 87

Eleutherius, 53
Encyclopaedia Britannica, 54, 75
Engelhard, 61, 62, 98, 99
Engelhusius, Theodoric, 21, 45
Erchempert, 57, 58
Eugenia, St, 59–60, 61, 96
Eulogium Historiarum, 26–7
Euphrosyne, St, 60, 99

Fauconpret, C., 85–6

Feminist movement, Pope Joan and
the, 9, 75–6, 82
Flores Historiarum, 22, 24
Flores Temporum, 19–21, 22, 45, 58,
59, 91
Folmar, Archdeacon, 99
Formosus, Pope, 37, 40
Francis of Assisi, St, 58
Franciscans, 58–9
Francklin, John Fairfax, 70

Gaufridus de Collone, 22, 31, 32
Gebehard, Abbot of Windberg, 98
Goethe (*Faust*), 84
Gotfrid of Viterbo, 15, 25
Gregory VII, Pope, 41
Gregory XII, Pope, 51
Gregory of Tours, 96
Grimoire, Pope Joan's, 34
Guglielma of Bohemia, 93
Guglielmites, 93–4

Hadrian II, Pope, 39, 53, 90–1
Hadrian VI, Pope, 51
Haemerlein, Felix, 20, 28, 33
Harding, Thomas, 25, 49, 65, 66,
70
Harpsfield, Nicholas, 66
Hasenmuller, Elias, 49
Henry IV, Emperor, 41–2
Henslowe, Philip, 84
Hermannus Januensis, 19
Hermannus Schafnaburgensis, 25
Higden, Ranulph, 24, 30
Hilaria (Apollinaria), St, 60, 63
Hildegund, St, 61–3, 96, 97, 98–100
Hincmar, Archbishop of Rheims,
39–40
Historia De Donne Famose ('H.S.'),
34, 69
Historia Erphesfordensis, 23
*History of Pope Joan and the Whores
of Rome*, 67–8
Hugolina, Blessed, 63
Hus, John, 25, 36, 80, 88

Ince, Richard, 89–90, 91
Innocent III, Pope, 58

Innocent IV, Pope, 59
Innocent VII, Pope, 30
Innocent VIII, Pope, 43–4, 49
Innocent X, Pope, 51

James, M.R., 68
James the Deacon, 61
Jean de Mailly, 16–18, 21, 41, 42, 45, 51, 58, 59, 72, 74, 79
Jewel, John, 25, 64–6, 70
Joachim of Fiore, 59, 93
Joan of Arc, 96
Johannes of Cremona, 25
John VII, Pope, 15, 23, 40–1, 54
John VIII, Pope, 23, 40, 54, 80
John X, Pope, 54
John XI, Pope, 55, 67, 75
John XII, Pope, 55, 67, 75
John XIV, Pope, 81
'John XV, Pope', 81
John XIX, Pope, 55, 80
John XX, Pope, non-existence of, 80–1
John XXI, Pope, 80–1
John XXII, Pope, 35, 59
John XXIII, Pope, 80
John XXIII, antipope, 36, 80
Justin Martyr, 46
Justinian, Emperor, 60

Kist, N.C., 53
Koberger, Anton, 32

Lafrery's Map of Rome, 46–7
Leibnitz, G.W., 73
L'Enfant, James, 36
Leo IV, Pope, 12, 14, 38–40, 53
Leo VI, Pope, 54
Leo IX, Pope, 41, 56–7, 58, 76
Leo X, Pope, 51
Leo of Ostia, 25, 27
Le Quien, Michel, 73
Liudprand of Cremona, 55–6, 65, 68
Lothair, Emperor, 14, 38, 39
Louis II, Emperor, 38, 39
Louvre Museum, Paris, 49–50
Lucius III. Pope, 100
Luther, Martin, 47, 48
Maifreda di Pirovano, 93–4
Mainz, 11, 14, 19–20
Mantuanus, Baptista, 28
Margaret of Antioch, St, 60
Margaret Reparata, St, 60, 61
Marianus Scotus, 14–15, 25
Marina, St, 60, 61
Marozia, 54–6, 67, 68, 75
Martin le Franc, 34
Martin Polonus, 11–13, 15–24, 26, 32, 44, 45, 47,
    Berlin manuscript of, 27, 29
    'John XV' and, 81
Martinus Minorita, 19
Matthew of Westminster, 22
Michael Cerularius, Patriarch of Constantinople, 41, 56, 76, 78

Mirabilia Urbis Romae, 27–8, 30, 46, 47
    Stephan Blanck's, 29, 31, 88, 91
Mitelli, Giuseppe Maria, 95
Mithraic memorials, 45–6
Moakley, Gertrude, 94
Monks, women, 59–63, 96, 98–100
Mosheim, John Laurence, 73, 74

Nicaea, Council of, 56, 57–8
Nicetas, Patriarch of Constantinople, 57–8
Nicholas I, Pope, 39–40
Nonnus, Bishop of Edessa, 61

Ordo Romanus, 51
Orelli, J.C. Von, 45
Otto, King of the Saxons, 55
Otto of Frisingen, 15, 25, 41

Paschal II, Pope, 17, 42, 51
Patrides, C.A., 97
Paul IV, Patriarch of Constantinople, 57
Pelagia, St, 61
Perrodo-Le Moyne, Henri, 76, 77, 81
Petrarch, Franceso, 29–30, 54, 87
Philip, Archbishop of Cologne, 62, 99
Photius, Patriarch of Constantinople, 40, 54, 77
Pierced seat, 31–33, 49–52, 53, 74, 79, 84
Pistorius, Johannes, 14
Pius II (Aeneas Sylvius Piccolomini), Pope, 64
Pius V, Pope, 49
Pius VI, Pope, 49, 52
Platina, Bartolomeo, 32, 50, 51, 64, 65
'Poope Jone' (play), 84
Pope Joan,
    assumed name of, 12, 17, 19–21, 75
    original name of, 12, 24–6
    number of, 22–3, 40–1
    place of birth, 19–21
    place of burial, 11, 16, 17, 27–8, 29, 30, 45
    son of, 27, 68, 74, 90
'Pope Joan' (card game), 95
Pope Joan, or an Account . . . ('R.W.'), 68
Pope Joan (film), 9, 86, 87
Poulson, Edward, 70–1
Present for a Papist, 68, 69
Protus and Hyacinth, SS, 60

Regino, 25
Revelation, Book of, 29, 54, 74
Rhöides, Emmanuel, 74, 86–8, 89, 91
Robert d'Usez, 31
Rolevinck, Werner, 23
Rome,

Greek School in, 34
'House of Pope Joan' in, 47
inscribed stone in, 16, 17–18, 30, 44–6
shunned street in, 11, 12, 19, 30, 43–44, 47, 48
statue in, 30–1, 44, 46–9
see also individual buildings
Rudolf of Wied, 99

Satan, Pope Joan in league with, 16–17, 26, 34, 83, 87
Scarperia, Jacobo d'Agnola di, 51
Schedel, Hartmannus, 13, 32, 33, 38
Schernberg, Dietrich, 26, 34, 83–4
Sedes Stercoraria, 50–1
Sergius III, Pope, 55
Settle, Elkanah, 84–5
Siena Cathedral, bust in, 34–5, 64, 79
Sigebert of Gemblours, 15
Simon Magus, 46
Sixtus V, Pope, 44, 47, 48
Spanheim, Frederic, 20
St John Lateran, 32–3, 43, 49–52,
    see also Pierced seat
St Peter's Basilica, 28, 29, 37, 39, 41, 43
statue, see Rome
Stephen of Bourbon, 16–17, 18, 21, 34, 41, 45, 51, 58, 59, 72
Stephen VII, Pope, 37
Stephen VIII, Pope, 54
street, shunned, see Rome
Summers, Montague, 85
Sylvester II, Pope, 34, 78–9
Sylvester IV, antipope, 42

Tegernesee manuscript, 25–6
Thecla, St, 61
Theodora, St, 60
Theodora, mother of Marozia, 54–6, 68
Theodora, sister of Marozia, 55, 56
Theodore II, Pope, 37
Theodoric, antipope, 42
Theodoric of Niem, 30, 31, 33–4, 47
Theophilus of Adana, 83
Theophylact, 54
Thomas of Malmesbury, 26–7
Thurston, Herbert, 62, 75
Tiraqueau, André, 34
Tolomeo of Lucca, 22–3, 40
Tomassetti, G., 47–8
Torrecremata, Cardinal, 65
Transvestism, Biblical ban on, 62
Trevisa, John de, 24

Ullman, Liv, 86
Uncumber (Wilgefortis), St, 60–1, 87
Unexplained, The, 54, 75
Urban II, Pope, 42
Urban III, Pope, 100

Van Maerlant, 18, 21
Vatican Museum,
  pierced seat in, 49–50
  statue in, 47–8
Vatican, secret archives of, 76, 77
Victor III, Pope, 42

Vincent of Beauvais, 79
Visconti-Sforza Tarot, 94

Waite, A.E., 95
Wilgefortis (Uncumber), St, 60–1, 87

William of Malmesbury, 78–9
William of Ockham, 35–6, 71
Wirth, Oswald, 95
Witekind, Hermann, 69
Wolfius, John, 28
Wood, Clement, 75, 78, 90–1